Diary of a Key West Innkeeper

Susan Jinbo

Phantom Press
Key West, Florida

Copyright 2006 Susan Jinbo

All rights reserved. Unauthorized duplication is a violation of applicable laws.

Reservations are strongly recommended. Check-in time is 2:00 p.m. - Check-out 11:00 a.m. All rates are based on availability and subject to change without notice. Cancellations must be made at least 24 hours in advance. Failure to cancel your reservation will result in floods, fires and catastrophic events.

All names and locations have been changed as a courtesy to the individuals involved, and in portions of the book dialogue has been added and composites used to better convey the events described.

Please address inquiries to:

info@phantompress.com

Cover Design: Jodi Bombace
Layout: Jodi Bombace
Editing: Mandy Bolen
Photos: Rob O'neal

ISBN:

ISBN 978-0-9789921-0-1

10 9 8 7 6 5 4 3 2 1

First Edition, Printed in the United States of America.

Diary of a Key West Innkeeper

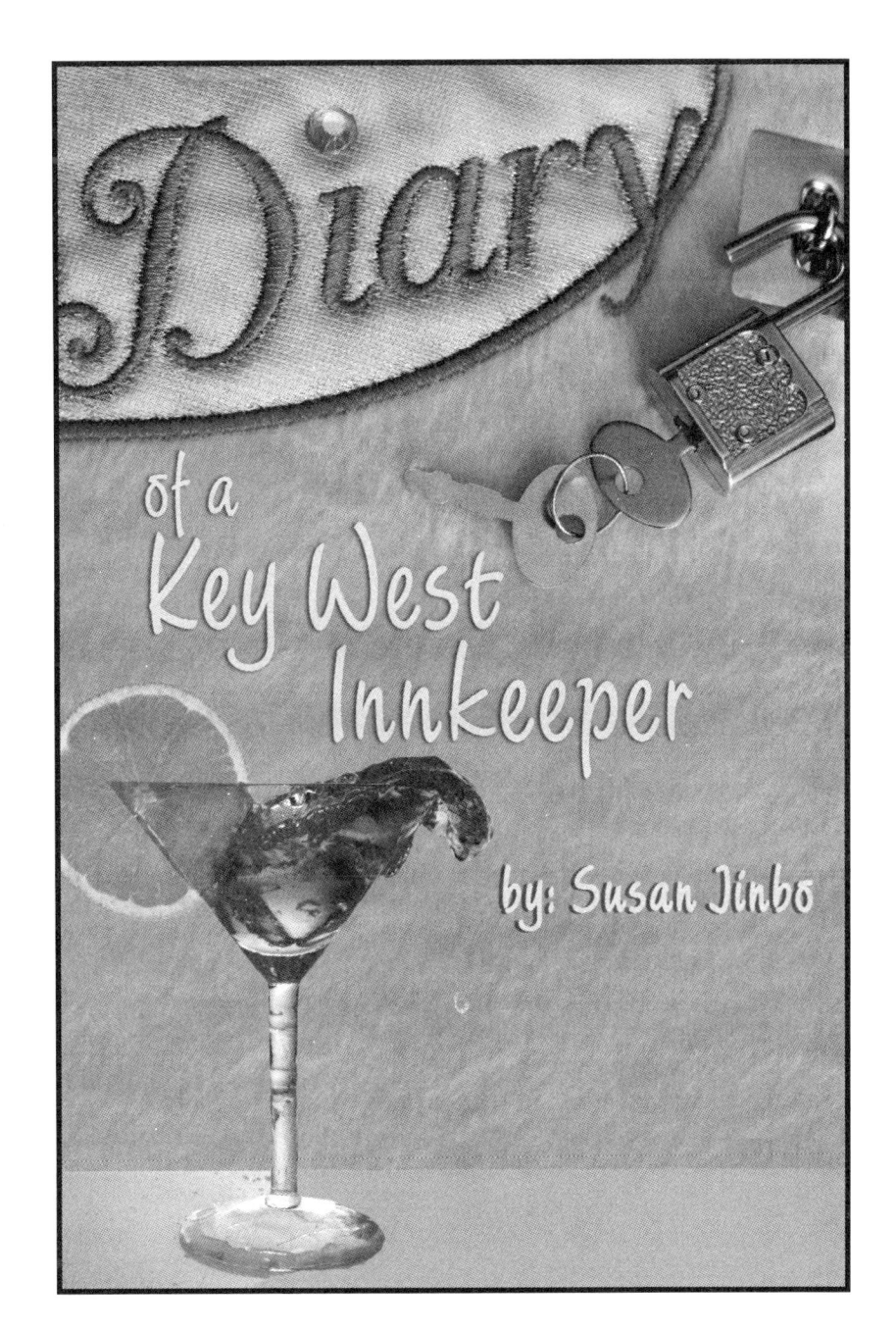

by: Susan Jinbo

Table of Contents

Prologue..1

In The Beginning..3

Oh My 11

Blacklist..17

Fire! Fire! Towel on Fire!.....................................24

The Death of a Legend..28

Joe-Joe the One-Armed Painter......................... 32

Animals...37

Lunch..42

New Friends.. 48

I Made a Fountain..52

Table of Contents

A Good Night's Sleep..58

Any Assistance is Appreciated............................65

Visiting Colleagues...73

Hurricane Charley...79

Black Flies..89

Jose Gato Diablo Snuggles...................................95

A Penny Saved...102

Fight Night..108

Should We Stay or Should We Go?..................113

Thank You..116

About the Author..118

Diary of a Key West Innkeeper

Prolouge

Photo courtesy of Jackie Dykhuizen

Prolouge

We were buying a guesthouse. A bed and breakfast. A small hotel. Whatever you called it, we were buying it. It was so exciting. We spent days and days tossing around our ideas and making lists. It would be beautiful. It would be a boutique hotel. People from around the world would clamor to stay in it.

We couldn't wait.

The current owner kindly offered to take us to a Key West Innkeepers Association meeting so that we could meet our soon-to-be colleagues.

The meeting was to be held, after hours, at a local bank. We expected speeches, useful information and an overall dry evening. I carried a pad of paper and a pen. I was ready to take notes.

We arrived a couple of minutes early. We opened the glass door to the bank. In the entry foyer, a table was set up to check everybody in. We gave our names and explained our circumstances: We were to be the new owners of Orchids! They smiled neutrally and gave us name-tags. I pressed mine carefully on my dress. My husband tossed his in the nearest trashcan. They were also selling raffle tickets. I bought too many, trying to fit in.

We entered the main lobby of the bank. Tables had been set up in a rough 'U' shape. They were weighted down with catered appetizers. The teller stations had been transformed into mini-bars. People were mingling, drinking, eating and laughing. We gaped in delighted surprise. These were our kind of people. I wanted to throw my arms wide and embrace them all.

At some point a couple of announcements were made and the raffle winners were announced. I didn't win, but I didn't care. I was glowing.

I left Craig chatting with an older guy who owned a hotel on the other side of the island and went up a deserted staircase to find the bathroom. I was preparing to flush when the door opened and I heard voices. I hesitated and listened. I realized they were talking about us.

"They seem so young!" one woman exclaimed.

"They do," the other woman agreed.

"She's very pretty," the first woman commented.

"Sure, but just wait till she's got a phone in one hand and a toilet plunger in the other. Bet she won't be so pretty then." They giggled. I chuckled silently along with them, laughing at their naivety. I would never have a toilet plunger in my hand.

I waited for them to leave before emerging from the stall, still chuckling. I sauntered down the deserted staircase, dreaming about our first movie star guest. I was hoping for Brad Pitt, but knew my husband was pulling for Elisabeth Shue.

When I re-entered the lobby, Craig was still in conversation. He met my eyes across the room. I could read his expression clearly, as I'm sure it was a reflection of my own. We smiled fondly at each other.

"This is going to be fun!"

In The Beginning

We bought Orchids Guesthouse the morning of August 27th, 2003. We'd had absolutely no training to be innkeepers, although we did have some lovely romantic dreams. The previous owner, Frank, a savvy businessman by any measure, had agreed to train us for seven days after closing, but had wisely declined even one minute of training before the deal was done. Having closed several properties in our lifetime, we'd expected to go through the tedious signing of a stack of documents orchestrated by a couple of attorneys and a closing agent and then... celebrate? But, of course, this was an ill-conceived notion. After all, we'd just spent well over a million dollars on an ongoing business. There were guests in the house and they now belonged to us. So we ran home under some pretense, toasted each other with a quick glass of cheap red wine and, full of anticipation, headed off to our new business.

It probably goes without saying that the night before we had not slept well. So, certainly, exhaustion was a factor on our first day. However, try to imagine the excitement of closing your new home and then running off to dig twenty or so holes in the dirt. That's how it felt. We were completely unprepared for the sheer physical labor involved with being innkeepers.

It started immediately. August in Key West is hot as hell even if you're outside under a shade tree with a lovely ocean breeze. Inside the un-air-conditioned common areas of the house where no breeze saw fit to visit, it felt like it was about 120 degrees with 100% humidity. It was like working in an oven. That first day we got there around one in the afternoon. There were seven loads of laundry to finish, fold, and put away on the third floor (with a 10-degree increase per floor). Dishes needed to be unpacked. The kitchen needed to be cleaned. The hallway needed to be mopped. The leaves needed to be swept up from the walkways and the back patio. The pools needed to be skimmed. The plants needed to be watered. Breakfast for the next morning needed to be prepped (God help me, this involved turning the stove on). Around 5 p.m. I felt we'd really put in a good afternoon of work, and surely it was time to go home. Frank looked at me with a mixture of amusement and sympathy.

"You have empty rooms tonight," he informed me softly.

"Yeah, I saw that. Let's hope for better tomorrow!" I exclaimed, forcing an optimistic note into my voice, trying to cover for my dead exhaustion.

"You don't go home until your rooms are filled," he said with a sly grin. "Or about nine o'clock tonight – whichever comes first."

In The Beginning

I stared at him blankly. Surely he was joking. Stay here for another four hours? In the off-chance that somebody just happened to wander by in search of a room? It seemed the pinnacle of insanity. Plus, I just didn't think I had it in me.

"Also," he continued, a certain amount of wicked satisfaction in his tone, "The laundry isn't done."

"How could it not be done?" I exclaimed. Good God Almighty! How much laundry could eight guestrooms produce? Slowly, through the sweat streaming into my eyes, through the aching of my arms and legs, through the slow burning need for a cold beer and a chair located anywhere with air-conditioning, the terrible answer occurred to me: An infinite amount. It was a shocking answer. All the more horrifying because I'd never thought to ask the question prior to that night.

"There's a comforter that still needs to go through," he continued.

I nodded, resigned. I didn't know where Craig was. Last I'd seen him, maybe an hour ago, maybe two, he'd been scrubbing a shower stall while Tammy, the previous owner's wife, stood behind him and offered up small criticisms. I didn't even want to think about what he might be doing now. Dirty toilet bowls and the brown sludge often found behind them came unbidden into my mind. I shuddered.

My dreams – of laughing gaily with smart, educated guests over a glass of wine in the evenings, of spending my afternoons relaxing in the sun and reading a book, of answering the phone pleasantly to people who wanted to be my guests – were crashing down around me in a matter of one day.

Craig and I finally went home that night just after 9 p.m. I don't remember being able to speak about it. It was terrible. The vastness of what we could only consider an enormous mistake was sinking in with crushing speed. In silence we stared at the TV, considered our options - and the lack thereof. Grimly, we got drunk and went to sleep.

The first few days passed in this way. We discovered how to maintain our reservation software, how to answer emails, how to update our vacancy information online so that it was available to other guesthouses that might have overflow, how to answer the phones without sounding like complete idiots, how to take a reservation and send out confirmations, how to make friends with the reservation agents around town who had possible guests for our vacancies, how to market the guesthouse and make advertising decisions, how to check-in arriving guests and how to answer at least a few of their million questions. While learning all of this we also perfected stripping rooms, which happened when a guest checked out and entailed removing every possible item and washing it while scrubbing what remained with a combination of chemicals that could induce a nosebleed. We figured out how to keep our pools from turning green and becoming a wildlife habitat. We got the hang of cooking a different breakfast every day for 16 people. And we managed to fold laundry while doing pretty much any and all of the above.

Then came the fourth day we owned Orchids. It had certainly occurred to us at this point that this was potentially a truly terrible job. But we had no idea how bad it could get.

We arrived that morning as the sun peeked up in the east, transforming the house from pitch black to the faded colors of dawn. The computer and phone – the lifelines of the business – were locked, as they should have been, in their cabinet. I poured water into the coffee-maker and deftly put the pot in its spot before the coffee started spilling out. This was no small trick, and one that had taken me three mornings to master. I felt a surge of confidence.

Craig went outside to sweep and I went to unlock the computer cabinet. There were two locks, top and bottom. The top lock was easy. But the bottom lock was stubborn and had a tendency to stick. Not to be bullied, I applied extra pressure to the lock. The key suddenly turned in my hand. It took me a moment to understand that I'd broken it. It took me another moment to understand that I'd broken it off in the lock. It took me even another moment to realize there was now no way to get to the computer. Or the phone.

As if on cue, the phone rang. I sat on the floor and stared at the half-key I held in my hand. Craig walked in and stopped beside me.

"You okay?" he asked, his tone wavering between pissed that I was taking an unscheduled break and concern that perhaps I'd finally had some sort of breakdown.

I held my hand out towards him, the key in my upturned palm. I didn't look at him, just continued to stare at the locked cabinet. It took him a second, but my husband's no fool. He quickly grasped the situation.

"Damn," he whispered reverently.

I nodded my head sadly.

"Let's get set up for breakfast – we'll deal with this later," he said decisively. It did seem to be our only option. I climbed to my feet and headed back into the kitchen.

The previous owners arrived shortly thereafter. Frank laughed heartily at the key mishap. "Six years I've had that cabinet, and never broken the key. You had it four days. Way to go Sue!"

I hated him.

I also couldn't help but notice that their sense of humor seemingly had some sort of inverse relationship with the number of days they had left to train us. As our number of days remaining together decreased, their sense of humor increased. This did nothing to cheer my mood.

I started in on breakfast. Frank, as had become our habit, hovered at my elbow and gave a running monologue of detailed instructions while I gritted my teeth and smiled. As the saying goes, this was a man who, if you asked him what time it was, would tell you how to build a clock.

"Slice the cantaloupe in half, then, meat side down, each half in half again. Then again...again...See, 16 even pieces! When you skin the piece, hold it like so...then use two fingers and pinch the skin away...don't separate the bananas before you peel them...slice them, then peel them together...that's it...angle the cheese grater a little more...good...now rotate the cheese as you grate it...don't hold the whisk that way...grip it like this..." and so on, and so on.

I'd fed maybe six or eight guests when Craig walked through the kitchen and shot me a stricken look. "What?" I mouthed at him, while smiling at a sleepy couple and describing, in my best cheerleader-on-crack voice, their upcoming breakfast. They listened patiently and agreed to the entire menu.

He waited while they helped themselves to some coffee and meandered towards the garden. On their way out the door, the woman turned back to me. "Susan, by the way, while it was raining last night, we had a lot of water come in through our ceiling. No big deal, we put towels down, just thought you should know."

"Great, thank you. Appreciate you letting us know." I grinned fiercely at her. Outstanding, we had a roof leak. I turned my attention back to Craig, who had gotten paler.

"We had a slip and fall last night," He finally told me dully.

"A what?"

"A slip and fall. In Bamboo Hideaway. They spent the night in the emergency room. She's got a bruised kidney."

Bamboo Hideaway was one of our two rooms in the back

cottage, both of which had outside entrances. Considering the rain in the night, it was not hard to believe that the old wooden steps to the room might have become slippery.

"Oh my god." I stared at him. Unbidden, tears welled in my eyes. I had a sudden, clear picture of us losing everything, and the lovely young couple staying in Bamboo Hideaway moving to Key West and taking over our guesthouse – which, of course, they would win in the lawsuit.

Tammy suggested tenderly that I might want to go outside for a moment and collect myself. I took her up on the offer, handing the spatula to Frank. I went outside into the misty morning, stood by the washing machine and wailed like a baby. Craig joined me after a couple of minutes, his eyes red, probably from his own private moment, perhaps at the garbage cans. We stared at each other. There was nothing to say.

I dried my eyes and we went back inside. Frank was offering juice to the injured woman and her boyfriend as they made their way to a breakfast table. I took over cooking and Frank and Craig huddled back outside, discussing options and making some quick decisions. I took breakfast out to the couple, tears still in my eyes. They felt terrible, you could tell. Probably not so terrible, mind you, that they wouldn't be looking for some money. But definitely really bad.

After breakfast, Craig took the boyfriend to the side and expressed our misery at the accident. He offered to comp their room for their whole stay and offered our insurance company information. The boyfriend took the room comp, but said he didn't think they'd need the insurance info. Then, with a quick glance at his watch, he thanked Craig for the free room and told him they had to get going or they were going to miss their snorkeling trip. Yes, that's right, their snorkeling trip. Out on the ocean. In the waves. On a boat. Yep.

Breakfast continued. The next guests were a sweet older couple from Minnesota, Lizzy and Chuck, who were traveling with their pink poodle. (Maria, our part-time cook and full-time housekeeper who seemingly had come with the property, was fascinated by the poodle, commenting frequently upon its particular shade of pink.) They were in the other cottage room, which happened to share a wall with the Bamboo Hideaway. As soon as they were seated in the gardens, a haunting cry echoed through the yard towards the house. It sounded like an old woman wailing at the grave side of her recently departed husband. There had been vague rumors of an Orchids ghost. Bleakly

In The Beginning

I wondered if perhaps she'd chosen this morning to introduce herself. Of course, it wasn't the ghost. It was the poodle, whose mournful cries were enough to set everyone's teeth on edge. I went into the garden where Lizzy and Chuck, both over eighty and deaf as doornails, sat enjoying their morning tea. I mentioned that the poodle was perhaps missing them, and maybe they should bring her out to join them for breakfast.

"What dear?" Lizzy asked, as a large leaf splashed into her teacup and she, not noticing, took a long sip.

I ignored the leaf and shouted the suggestion again.

"Oh, I don't think that's necessary," she answered sweetly.

"She's making a bit of noise!" I yelled, while not just my own guests, but guests from the hotel next door turned their heads to stare. I could only imagine how pleased the neighboring guests were that they'd chosen a guesthouse were the owners didn't holler at them over breakfast.

"Oh! I'm sorry. Let me get her." Lizzy tottered off towards the room while I pondered the idea that the injured guest would return from her snorkeling adventure in search of some peace and quiet only to have a howling pink poodle for a neighbor. Lovely.

I returned to the kitchen. Tammy stopped me before I got to the stove. She put a firm hand on my arm.

"A cooler was being defrosted in the Magnolia Room and the water has run down into the Fisherman's Retreat." She spoke slowly and firmly.

"Oh great, what were they doing defrosting a cooler on the floor?" I asked crossly.

"It's okay, now," she continued, in the same measured tones. "We've cleaned it up."

"Thanks," I offered lamely, not really caring. I was later informed that a "cooler" spilling on the floor was code for a toilet overflowing. Apparently, the guests in the room below took a more favorable view on a leak if they didn't have reason to believe there might be human sewage involved. Right.

The day went on.

Amazingly.

Our two vacant rooms were filled by the reservation agents whose asses I'd been puckering up to for the past four days. Craig went to our house for his power drill and managed to drill the bottom lock out of the computer cabinet so that we could at least open it and lock it with the top lock.

One of our guests, upon checkout, informed me that they thought I'd be a great innkeeper if I just "relaxed and took it down a notch or two."

And at the end of the day, while Craig and I sat on our couch drinking wine as if someone were paying us to do it and our dogs watched in barely disguised alarm, we fell into hysterical laughter with tears streaming down our cheeks. "So," Craig managed through his giggles, "You wanted to buy a guesthouse."

Oh My ...

Of course we had studied the financials of the business prior to purchasing it. Obviously. We even had a friend who did that sort of thing for a living take a look. Okay, we disregarded her advice. But we knew better. We were smart people who could see that while the guesthouse was no gold mine, it did make money.

So it was a somewhat alarming discovery at the end of the first month of operations that we had overlooked one significant fact: we had not figured on paying ourselves. And the small profit margin that we'd felt pretty smug about just weeks ago wouldn't begin to cover the second mortgage on our personal home, no less our wine and cigarette habit. Even food, it appeared, would be out of the question.

There was only one thing to do. We had to cut the hours of the one person who was keeping us sane. And do her job ourselves. In addition to our other jobs.

During our training sessions with the previous owners, while I was learning the exact spacing of the coffee cups as determined with a ruler and Craig was being introduced to the intricacies of toilet handle polishing, Maria had passed by me and whispered, "Is no problem, I show you better. Is easy."

Did I hear her correctly? Anxiously, I waited for a moment alone with my husband to pass this along.

"What do you think she meant?" he asked in a hushed, eager tone.

"I'm not sure," I whispered back to him, glancing over my shoulder to be sure we were alone.

"If there's an easier way..." he let the thought hang there, like the promised land, dangling just out of our reach.

Seven days after the purchase, Frank wished us luck, gave us a wave, and walked laughing out the front door.

The phone rang, my stomach clenched, and I answered it alone for the first time. It was some woman wanting rates for New Year's. How the hell was I supposed to know? I panicked, quoted nearly $70 per night less than I should have, and she promptly made the reservation. Blissfully, it would be nearly two months before I realized my mistake. I found Craig watering the plants and informed him in a self-satisfied voice about the seven-night stay I had just booked. He high-fived me. Looked like we just might make it.

Maria walked by with a load of folded towels in her arms and smiled at us. "You do good," she told me confidently. When Maria said 'you' it sounded like 'jew', as 'Y's' were not her strong suit. I nodded in cheerful agreement.

"Want some help on the rooms?" Craig asked her. She looked at him quizzically. "You want?"

"Sure!" It was a good day. Birds were chirping, the sun was shining, reservations were coming in and we were going to be fine. They went off to get started on make-ups (which, for those of you happy enough to not know, means cleaning a room when the guest is staying over). I went to the computer to proudly enter my new reservation.

A little over an hour later, Maria had finished six rooms and Craig had not reappeared from his first. She went to check on him. I was busy answering emails, but was still mildly concerned that he had not shown back up. I heard Maria's laughter echoing down the staircase.

Craig told me later that Maria had found him in the shower stall, scrubbing it down. The previous owner's wife had taught him how to do make-ups. Unfortunately, she had never actually done one because Maria worked full-time. As a result, and not wanting to appear incompetent, she'd taught him to strip the room exactly as he would for an incoming guest. While admirable, it was completely unrealistic.

Maria taught both of us how to do a make-up.

"Five things," she said, wriggling her fingers in front of our attentive faces.

"One, Make bed. Two, take garbage. Three, new towels. Four, soap. Five, face tissue." She smiled broadly at us. "That's it!" She threw her hands in the air. We wanted to hug her.

Soon, Maria started making small changes to the rooms. The previous owners had been big fans of doilies. They made for a dusting nightmare and put a person immediately in mind of their grandma's house. One day, Maria came up to me at the desk, holding a stained doily that had maybe at one time been white.

"You like?" she asked, wrinkling her nose so as there was no doubt to the correct answer.

"No," I answered, which was true. But she could have been holding up a Picasso and I would have gladly thrown it in the trash to keep her happy. "You?"

"No. Is cuchino." She cocked her head at me to see if I understood.

"I don't know cuchino," I told her.

"Cuchino, cuchino," she repeated, perhaps working under the assumption that repetition in a loud impatient voice would improve my non-existent Spanish skills.

She stamped her foot; she hated the language barrier. "Greg!" she yelled. She called my husband Greg as she couldn't pronounce the "Cr" combo.

He answered back from somewhere upstairs. "Como se dice cuchino en Ingles," she shouted towards him.

"Dirty," the reply floated down.

"Is dirty. Dirty. You see?"

"Cuchino," I agreed, trying out the word.

She smiled proudly at me. I grinned back. "Dirty," she said again, pronouncing it carefully.

"Yes, cuchino."

Maria got bolder as the weeks passed. All of the things that had driven her crazy for the past seven years as a housekeeper were now up for grabs. They were giddy times.

There was a shelf that went around the entire kitchen and was overflowing with the knick-knacks and junk the previous owners just couldn't bear to part with. One morning we arrived and the shelf was empty. "If You Like Pina Coladas" was playing on the radio and Maria was singing along, loudly and quite off-key.

"Buenas dias Senorita!" Craig greeted her heartily as we walked in.

"Hola amigos!" she shouted back.

"What happened?" I pointed at the shelf. I was a little shocked and therefore felt justified in bypassing the pleasantries.

"I clean. You like?"

"Sure. Yeah. It's great!" I smiled brightly and tried to match her enthusiasm. "But where's all the stuff?"

"Is okay. You decide." She gestured out the side door at the laundry area, that I now saw was covered in the junk from the shelves. Apparently, she just couldn't wait for me to get around to sorting it out in my own sweet time.

I went outside and started to inventory the items, creating three piles: Definite Garbage, Possible Garbage and Keepers. The Definite Garbage pile quickly made the other piles look small and meager. Amongst other items, it included three dusty stuffed animals that were probably won throwing darts at a county fair, seven baskets with either holes or broken handles, a small square box full of cigarette ashes, a plastic snow globe from Walgreens and a collection of chipped dishes. A month or so later, when the previous owner stopped by to say hello (and gloat), he noticed the missing shelf of junk.

Oh My ...

"When did you clean that off?" he asked, alarmed.

"A while ago. Looks great, don't you think?" I smiled fondly at the bright empty space.

"Did you come across a box of ashes?"

Noting his concerned tone and clearly able to picture said box lying in the Definite Garbage pile, I lied. "No, nothing like that. Why?"

"Oh no. My wife's going to be so sad."

"Why?"

"Those were the cremated remains of our beloved cat. Are you sure you didn't find them?"

"No, sorry." I was wide-eyed and earnest. The picture of sincerity. Of course I felt bad. But, in my defense and with no offense to the memory of what I'm sure was a lovely pet, how the hell was I supposed to know?

Junk around the house had been the bane of Maria's existence for too long, and she could smell the change in the air. The garbage cans overflowed - it was like a festival.

So, when the end of the first month rolled around and the financial information hit the fan, our decision to cut Maria's hours was a terrible one.

We struggled with it night after night, rehashing the income versus expenses, reluctant to admit even to each other that we could have so grossly miscalculated. When there was finally no other explanation and no other alternative, we worked out a twenty-hour per week schedule for Maria. I typed it up on a neat spreadsheet. I color-coded it. If I'd thought it was appropriate, I would have added a pink heart border. She would now work five days a week, four hours a day. What was left unfinished, which would be significant, we would do ourselves.

We went to the guesthouse the next morning with heavy hearts. After breakfast, Craig started the rooms. "We talk?" I asked Maria, indicating the kitchen table.

I pulled out my miserable spreadsheet, wishing I'd added the border. "We have some money problems," I started, speaking slowly and clearly and emphasizing with my hands. "We are going to need you to work fewer hours."

She stared at me for a minute, her eyes filling with tears. "You no like my work?" she finally said.

"No, no!" I exclaimed. "You're work is great. It's the money." I rubbed my fingers together in the universal sign of money. She nodded slowly. I pushed the spreadsheet towards her.

She stared at the paper for a moment, then flipped it over and started writing.

"This is what I do," she informed me briskly, all sign of tears gone. She passed the paper back to me and I looked down at her new schedule. It was for roughly forty hours. She leaned over and kissed me on the cheek. "I think so I love you too much," she told me and smiled broadly.

Now I was teary. "I love you too!" I exclaimed, hugging her across the table.

"I clean my kitchen," she told me, standing up.

"Thank you." I blew her a kiss and went to find my husband. He was doing the make-up in Hibiscus Room.

"How'd it go?" he asked me.

I handed him Maria's new schedule and shrugged apologetically.

He stared at it for a moment. "Ramen noodles it is."

"People have survived on less," I agreed.

He nodded, silent.

"With some chopped green onions..." I faded off.

He resumed making the bed and I moved to the other side to help. My mind was racing. Surely, this could be worse. After all, Ramen noodles were delicious. There were four flavors and you could add stuff. Mushrooms, red peppers, frozen peas...maybe even chicken for a special occasion. Everything was going to be okay. I smiled confidently in his direction. My husband collected the garbage and headed out of the room.

Blacklist

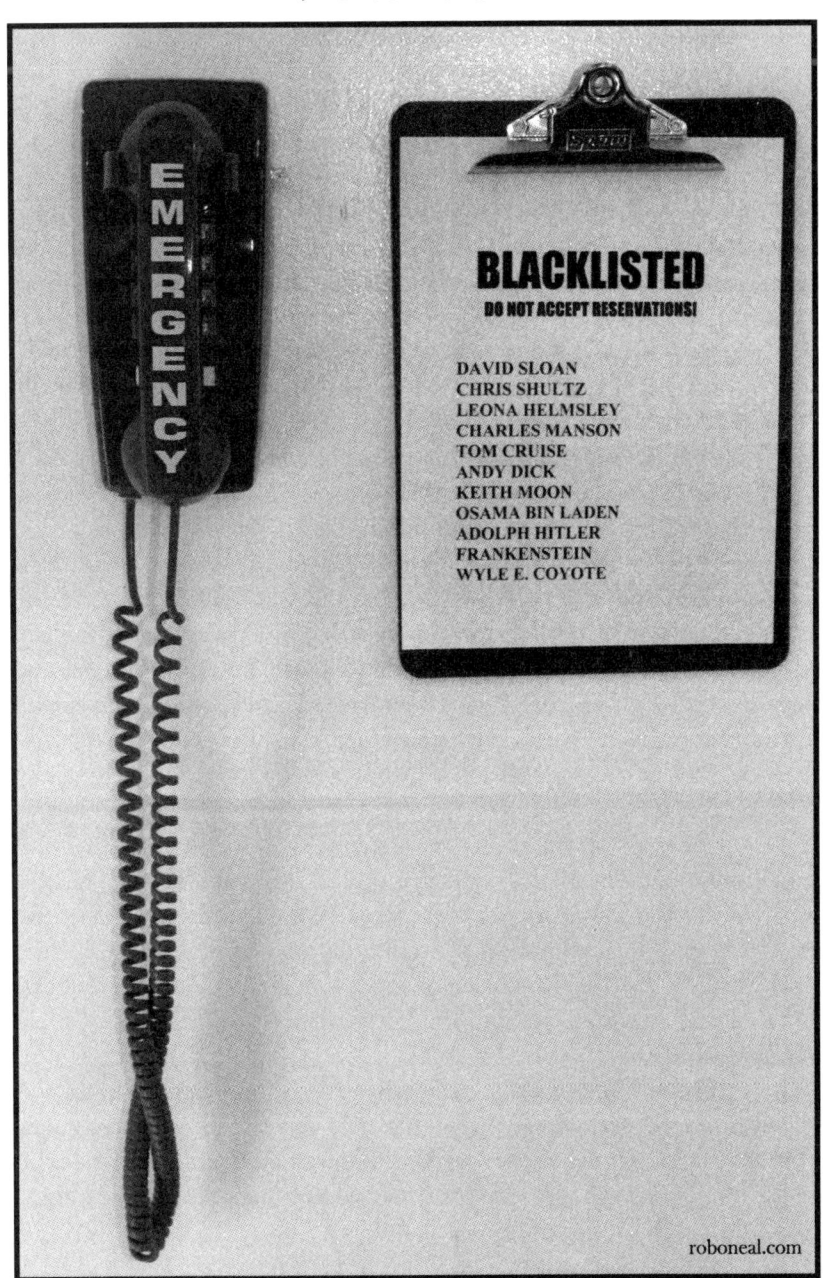

BLACKLISTED
DO NOT ACCEPT RESERVATIONS!

DAVID SLOAN
CHRIS SHULTZ
LEONA HELMSLEY
CHARLES MANSON
TOM CRUISE
ANDY DICK
KEITH MOON
OSAMA BIN LADEN
ADOLPH HITLER
FRANKENSTEIN
WYLE E. COYOTE

roboneal.com

She was the first guest that we put on our blacklist. It was a fairly difficult place to land. The aging diabetic southern belle with the insincere smile who had to have special breakfast items cooked to order and accompanied by three pancakes and extra syrup did not make the list. Nor did the massively overweight bride who needed our mixing bowls to soak her swollen ankles and then needed us to stand by with polite smiles while she lectured us on her suggestions for building and business improvements. Nor did the Fantasy Fest couple who used the hot tub to wash off body paint. Even the young gay couple who accidentally killed $450 worth of fish in our pond, locked themselves out of their room at midnight, and, as we discovered one morning upon arrival, were running an impromptu massage business in the backyard at 3 a.m. were not, believe it or not, actually blacklisted.

But to her full credit, and in the face of some fairly steep competition, Victoria managed to eek out the illustrious position of First Guest on the Blacklist. It started upon her arrival.

Admittedly, the roof work that was slated to be complete before we re-opened for guests had run behind schedule due to unexpected torrential rains in the middle of the dry season. Our luck was nothing if not consistent.

The day Victoria arrived, there was still a considerable amount of banging from the roofers - six or eight men with questionable eyes and dirty laughs. Maria had overheard them talking and repeated a couple of key phrases to me. That's how I knew their eyes were questionable and their laughter dirty. It was also a chilly day, cloudy, gray, and spitting rain from time to time.

I greeted Victoria. I was wearing Key West winter gear, due to an unseasonable cold spell that had accompanied the rain. It was a terrible mix of leftover cold weather clothing layered with absolutely no consideration of coordinating or even fitting (the cordouroy pants were my husband's, held up by a piece of string as I hadn't been able to locate a belt.) But it beat freezing, and you'd be surprised how cold sixty degrees can get with no heat.

"Hello! Welcome!" I greeted her with a forced enthusiasm. Victoria looked around the hallway, a little messy from the continuing efforts to put the house back together, then settled her gaze on me. Her eyes, mean and small, peered out of the layers of fat on her face. I could count the pores on her nose.

"Sooozy!" The cry floated down from the roof. This had been going on for the two weeks of our emergency shut-down, and had my nerves raw. One of the workers, who was not completely right in the head, had apparently been jilted by a woman named Suzy. About a hundred times a day he would cry out her name. It was spooky – like a solitary loon calling across a foggy lake at dawn.

"I sincerely hope this is not going to continue while I'm here," she stated flatly.

"Oh no, they're almost done." My smile was as hard and bright as a shiny new penny.

Victoria appeared unconvinced, but she nonetheless reluctantly surrendered her credit card to pay for her three-night stay. I checked her in, going through my little routine about the house like a hard-core cheerleader determined to move the crowd. It was to no avail. While I did this, Craig gallantly moved her seven suitcases into the Magnolia Room, a large romantic room on the second floor. He had to haul them up the staircase one by one as Victoria had evidently seen fit to bring her pet rock collection along for her short trip. I took her up to the room behind Craig as he struggled with the last of the luggage. Victoria managed an expression of extreme inconvenience over the delay on the steps.

"This will do," she informed me inside the room, after a long look around that reminded me of a bulldog checking out her new digs. I half expected her to lift her leg and piss on the corner of the bed.

"Great!" I smiled again and backed out of the room with a sigh of relief.

Downstairs, Craig and I sat to have a cigarette and bitch a little about the new arrivals. Maria passed us on her way to sweep the upper hallway.

"No judge first day, grumpy! We change." She smiled confidently, her brown eyes twinkling, and kept walking. She was right, we acknowledged, many of our guests started out terrible after just leaving the stress of their lives and traveling for eight or ten hours. Generally, an evening in Key West plus a good night's sleep changed all of them for the better.

Twenty minutes later, the rain started again. The workers scurried off the roof as if deserting a sinking ship. Work would finish tomorrow, fingers crossed and weather finally, please God, permitting.

We went back to work. I can't remember if we were unloading dishes or folding a load of towels, when Maria reappeared.

"I no love too much the big ugly face woman," she informed us, the twinkle missing from her eye.

"Maria!" I admonished, glancing towards the hallway to make

sure Victoria was not in hearing distance. I repeated Maria's own lecture about waiting to judge a guest, in slightly less broken English.

"Okay," she agreed. "Tomorrow I cook a beautiful breakfast, with lots of love and cyanorra."

I nodded and smiled.

"You know where I get cyanorra?" she asked innocently.

"No...what is cyanorra?"

She repeated the word for me several times, falling back on her assumption that repetition somehow helped me bridge the language barrier. Finally, she mimed eating off a plate, then grabbed her throat dramatically, stuck out her tongue, and pretended to die on the table.

"Cyanide!" my husband shouted happily, as if he'd just won at charades.

Maria grinned appreciatively. It was big fun for all of us when we managed to add a new word to her vocabulary.

I sobered quickly and told Maria that there would be no cyanide for breakfast - I didn't really think she'd do it, but this was the first guest that she had suggested poisoning. I didn't want to run any risks.

"Why do you want to poison her?"

"Big ugly face woman need mucho extra towel. She not even shower. Just need." Craig was laughing at the name-calling while I watched down the hall with my typical paranoia.

"How many towels?" I asked, thinking an extra towel was no big deal.

"Whole set - six extra! She no even say thank you!" she exclaimed.

It was a lot; I had to admit - especially for a woman who had yet to take a shower.

"Maybe her gorda body need extra to dry," Maria continued.

We managed to wrap up the conversation with everybody in halfhearted agreement that extra towels were not the end of the world and perhaps the woman's disposition would improve tomorrow. It felt empty and overly optimistic.

The next morning Craig and I arrived just after nine, as was our habit. Maria had cooked a beautiful breakfast, thankfully lacking any cyanide.

Craig and I quickly lost track of each other after breakfast, as our morning routines didn't cross often. I was responding to e-mail reservation requests when Victoria planted herself beside my desk.

"Good morning!" I nearly shouted at her.

"How am I supposed to take a shower with no curtain on the window. Those workers are all over the roof. And you said they'd be done yesterday."

I took it one item at a time. "Well, unfortunately, the workers got delayed again because of the rain. They will finish today. It's going to be a beautiful day. And if you need something over the window, we'll be happy to put up a curtain."

"You said they'd be done yesterday," she grunted, like the bulldog she was.

"Right, but it rained."

"I work seven days a week as a very important attorney in Orlando, and I don't get away often. I think you should have told me when I made my reservation this would be going on."

"We didn't know. They got delayed." I felt my patience ebbing and the smile sliding off my face. My hands started to shake a little, a physical reaction I have to getting mad. It's annoying as hell. "Believe me, Victoria, this is not our choice either. We would have loved for the roof to finish on time."

"I'm very dissatisfied with this," she said, glaring at me, "My room is right next to the banging."

"You're welcome to leave. I will happily give you a refund for your remaining nights." I said a silent prayer that she would take me up on it.

"I don't want to spend the next three hours trying to find a new place to stay."

"I can move you to another room. I have two lovely rooms open that would be in the front of the house, away from the banging." Out of the corner of my eye, I saw my husband slide by into the kitchen with the plunger in his hand. He looked ready to murder somebody. I knew the feeling.

"I don't want a new room. I want that room." So this was the gist of it. She wanted money.

"Victoria, I'm trying to find a solution to your problem. You just say no to everything I suggest. What would you suggest?" I knew damn well what she would suggest, I just didn't want to help her by mentioning it first.

"I don't know, I just know I'm very unhappy."

"I don't know what to do for you, Victoria. I'll put a curtain over your window and the workers have assured me they'll be done, completely, before noon."

"I think it would be only fair for you to discount my room." There, she'd finally said it.

"What do you think would be a fair discount for these three hours of discomfort?" I asked, trying to will a reasonable tone of voice.

"I don't know," she repeated.

"How about ten percent off your stay?" I offered.

She made a rude snorting sound. "What is that, $13 per night?"

"Roughly, yes."

"That's not going to make me happy," she stated flatly.

"Okay, how about $20 per night for all three nights."

She seemed to ponder this offer, but it was an act. She had known all along what she wanted and was just making a show of thinking it through. "I think $100 per night would be reasonable," she finally spit out.

I thought about it for a second, then told her I'd have to discuss that large of a discount with my husband first. I'd get back to her.

I found Craig in the kitchen, sitting at the table with Maria. They both looked glum. They were talking in hushed tones.

"What's up?" I asked as I entered.

Craig shuddered. "I just had to plunge Magnolia Room's dump."

It is often our habit to refer to our guests by their room. Often, particularly in times of high turnover, it's impossible to quickly remember names. And sometimes, you just don't want to.

"Her toilet stopped up?" I asked, trying to clarify.

"Yes, it stopped up. Then that bitch took a dump in it. A big, messy dump. Then she called me to come in and plunge it. I think I'm going to be sick." With these words Craig jumped up from the table and ran for the staff bathroom. We could hear him heaving.

"She a nasty woman. Nasty. Nasty." Maria said this, repeating what was obviously a new word several times. If you gave Victoria credit for nothing else, you'd have to admit she was doing a fine job of expanding our housekeeper's vocabulary.

Craig returned from the bathroom looking pale. I informed him of Victoria's request for a discount and a curtain. I pulled the kitchen door shut, a rare act, to keep any of the guests from hearing the explosion of cursing.

"Maria," he started, after regaining a small semblance of control. "Find me the ugliest sheet we have. I'll go up, fix her window, and discuss her discount."

Craig got the ladder and the staple gun, took the purple and pink flowered sheet from Maria, and headed upstairs. I decided to follow, fearing the confrontation to come.

Victoria answered the door in a skimpy bathrobe that I speculated might bring a new onslaught of Craig's nausea. She sat on the bed and stared at the TV, which had not been shut off as far as we could tell since her arrival. It raised the obvious question of why a person would come all the way to Key West to order in food and watch TV. Craig and I set up the ladder and he went about viciously stapling the sheet to the window. I wondered briefly how we would get it down later. I didn't interrupt him to ask. When he finished, he took a deep breath and joined Victoria in the bedroom. He placed himself squarely in front of the TV.

"Susan has told me about your request," he stated. Victoria started to say something, most likely her litany about how unhappy she was, but Craig overrode her attempt to talk. "Let me tell you what I am willing to do. I will give you this room for $100 tonight, one night only, due to the construction that is happening today."

Craig is the king of negotiating. He doesn't leave any door open for further discussion. The amazing thing was that Victoria smiled and thanked him. It occurred to me that she was the kind of woman who liked to push other women around. Either that, or she, regardless of her high-powered job, couldn't add. Because she had obviously turned down my offer of three nights discounted at $20 each in favor of my husband's one-time $30 discount.

As we left the room, Victoria asked us to bring her some extra towels. I went to the closet and returned with a stack. When she answered the door, one huge flaccid breast threatened to escape the confines of her bathrobe. I averted my eyes and handed her the towels.

Two days later I said goodbye to Victoria. Craig and Maria had made themselves conspicuously scarce just in time for the farewells. Victoria shook my hand and thanked me for a lovely stay. Then with the air of a priest bestowing a blessing, she vowed to come back again next year. I smiled brightly, thanked her, and promptly learned how to use the "blacklist" function on our computer.

Fire! Fire! Towel on Fire!

Maria had five distinct ways to pronounce my name. All but one of them were with two sharply separate syllables and two hard S's.

"Soo-san," in a loud whisper meant she had something secret to show or tell me. Improperly disposed of used condoms is a good example.

"Uh...Soo-san." This was her business mode, spoken quickly and always preceded with the "Uh" as if in her hurry to impart the need for three new mattress covers my name temporarily escaped her.

"Soo-San!" High pitched and excited. Something good had happened, such as the arrival of a new stray cat or one of the orchids coming into bloom.

"Soozan," spoken low and dragged out. Reserved for when she thought I'd done something funny but inherently wicked.

And the emergency. "Soo San! Soo San!"

I was responding to an e-mail. Trying to sound clever and attentive while answering a list of nine questions sent in by a potential reservation. I was also trying not to lie outright while still keeping her interested. It was a thin line to walk.

I was deep in concentration, scowling at the computer screen while describing our small pool in response to question #6 - "A lovely place to get wet and relax in the afternoon with a cocktail, you can't swim laps, but you're on vacation, so who wants to work that hard! HA! HA!" In the background I could hear guests laughing in the garden over breakfast, our bird chirping, and an insistent beeping. I moved on to question #7.

"Do you have a cocktail hour?" Sure, depending on the day it can last from noon forward. Hmm...Maybe not the right answer. I pondered and started to type.

"SOO SAN! SOO SAN!" Maria came running at the desk. "Follow me!" she yelled, waving her arm over her head as if we were getting ready to secure a hill. I jumped up and followed.

She dashed through the kitchen and out the side door. The beeping that had barely registered with me moments before was growing louder. She ran towards the back cottage.

The door to the Bamboo Hideaway was locked but there was now no doubt that the beeping was coming from inside. And it was loud. I still didn't know what it was.

Maria whipped out her keys and threw the door open. Flames jumped from a towel that had been hung over the center light fixture towards the old wooden boards of the cathedral ceiling. With the door

Diary of a Key West Innkeeper

open, the fire alarm was wailing.

I screamed like a little girl who'd spotted a rat. I jumped back and waved my hands in the air. If there had been a stool nearby, I'm sure I would have leapt on it.

Maria ran into the room and up the stairs that led to its loft. After years of dusting the light fixture, she knew exactly which step allowed her to reach it.

She grabbed the towel from the top of the chandelier and ran like an Olympic champion in the flag-dancing competition (okay, probably not what it's called but you know what I'm talking about) with it held high above her head and flames dancing behind her. Down the steps and out the door. A couple of graceful turns and she dumped it outside on the small deck. I came to life. Better late than never. I ran for the kitchen and grabbed the coffee to put out the fire. I passed one of our state required extinguishers along the way, but figured this was not the time to read the instructions and learn how to use it.

Panting, we stood shoulder to shoulder, staring at the blackened smouldering towel. The fire alarm finally stopped. I looked at Maria. I thought of what would have happened if she hadn't been in the kitchen and heard and recognized the alarm. The sprinkler system would have gone off. Thousands upon thousands of dollars of water damage. My hands were shaking.

We walked back into the room. The smoke was thick and dark. The current guests were due to check out. We had a new guest arriving at about 3 p.m. that afternoon. Without a word, we opened the windows and propped open the door. Then we walked back to the breakfast tables, where nobody had noticed a thing, and located the man who had rented the room and seen fit to catch it on fire.

He was holding court with some other guests, telling a story. Everyone was laughing. His flowing bleach-blonde hair with red highlights glowed under the morning sun.

"Good morning," I interrupted him, for once forgoing my cheerleader smile.

"Susan!" he hailed jovially. "A good morning to you!"
Maria stood at my elbow, glaring.

"Chuck, you have caught your room on fire," I informed him. I could see no easier way to break the news.

His smile faltered. Was this a joke?

"We've put out the fire, but we've left your room open to let it air out."

"Oh my God. What happened?"

"You draped a towel over the light fixture. It caught fire."

Maria, quivering at my side with barely concealed fury, could no longer contain herself.

"Why you do that? Why you do that?"she cried out.

"I wanted it to dry out," he informed us blankly.

"Estupido!" she said to me, but in a voice that was intended to and did carry to the whole table. She continued as if they weren't there.

"You know 'estupido'?"

"Yes," I answered her, nodding. My Spanish was improving at a pretty slow rate, but even I understood the gist of 'estupido'.

Maria stomped back into the kitchen and started loading the dishwasher, the angry clash of dishes audible to where we all stood silent. You would have thought it was her house that nearly burned down. Then again, maybe in some ways, it was.

The man excused himself and went towards the room. I heard him on his cell phone, contacting his lawyer.

They checked out an hour later, apologizing profusely. His girlfriend sprayed her cheap perfume liberally around the room to try to cover the smoke smell. The smell of that combination is nearly impossible to describe. Needless to say, it added to our problems.

They left a $5 tip for Maria, well below average even if you haven't caught your room on fire. Craig returned home from grocery shopping. He gallantly overcame his irritation that nobody came to help unload the groceries when he heard about our morning. It took all three of us two hours to clean the room. Still the smoke smell lingered mixed with the sick-sweet smell of her perfume. But sometimes, even at a guesthouse, you get lucky.

The new guests were smokers, and never noticed.

Diary of a Key West Innkeeper

Death of a Legend

In Key West, cats roam the island like royalty. They wander in and out of any yard they choose, and often any house as well. If they like you, they settle down and wait expectantly for breakfast. We had four cats at the guesthouse, most of which came to us in this way. Maria was a lover of any living animal, but cats were her particular soft spot. Every time a new stray showed up she would promptly name it and offer it a bowl of tuna fish. Our cats were "Yellow," because it was yellow; "Black Cat" – that's right, a black cat; "Sweet Pea" – a huge beautiful Tabby with a temperament that could convince any feline hater to change their ways; and "Fred" – an ornery, ugly, scarred old tom cat who ruled the other cats through howling cat fights that usually, to our guests' delight, took place in the hallways of the house between 2 a.m. and 5 a.m.

Smokey, an old, gray long-haired cat of the famous six-toed Hemingway variety, actually belonged to the hotel next door, where his name was Big. I don't know if it was the Chicken-of-the-Sea albacore tuna (in water, not oil) that Maria fed him every morning or if it was Maria's own brand of love, but Smokey spent his days at Orchids. And everybody loved Smokey.

One day, I put out fresh water for him because he seemed thirsty and unhappy with the "stale" water in his bowl. Nina, our sweet, part-time front desk person whom we'd recently hired in defeated acceptance of our need for a day off, walked by me as I put the bowl of fresh water down on the deck. She was singing softly.

"Niles sales and service, we make buying a car so easy. Niles sales and service, we always go the extra mile at Niles." Our radio played all day long at the guesthouse. Nina had moved to America recently from England and apparently the jingles stuck in her head a lot easier than the songs.

"Smokey only likes running water," she informed me absently, pausing mid-song, as she sauntered past and waived absently at a mosquito. "Hold him over the kitchen sink so that he can drink from the faucet."

I stared at her for a moment, taken aback. She stopped, suddenly nervous, and covered her mouth with her hand as if she had said something she shouldn't have. Which, of course, she had.

"I don't want to know how you know that," I finally said.

"I'm just guessing?" she suggested tentatively.

"Do not water Smokey in the kitchen sink," I said firmly, after another pause, trying unsuccessfully not to laugh. "Just don't do it," I added in what I hoped would pass for an authoritative voice. All we'd need is for the state health inspector to show up while Nina had a cat hung over the kitchen sink, patiently waiting for him to drink his fill.

While everybody obviously loved and spoiled Smokey, it was Maria who loved him best. Another day, I came into work and there was a four-inch scratch across Maria's chest.

"What happened?" I exclaimed.

"Is nothing," she told me smiling. "I think so I love Smokey too much. I pick him up," and here she started pantomiming her actions, "and I hug him and I kiss him," she kissed the air above her cradled arms. "Then Smokey decide maybe I hug him too much, so he," lacking the word, she growled and scratched the air. "Is okay, though," she continued matter-of-factly, "I fine." She smiled glowingly at me.

I was reminded of a story Maria's husband, Angelo, told us when he was visiting a couple of months earlier. Angelo had a pet cockatiel when he met Maria and they started dating. He had always been a friendly bird, so Angelo was surprised when, after the first few times Maria had been to his house, the bird would hiss and back away from the bars of his cage every time she entered the room. One day, upon arriving home, Angelo noticed the bird had red spots across his feathers. At this point in the story, Maria, who was sitting nearby, started laughing heartily.

"What happened to the bird?" Craig asked.

Maria took over the narration. "I try and I try make friends with that bird. Every day, I get him out of his cage and I kiss him and I tell him 'I your friend, I your friend'." Maria kissed the air eight or ten times quickly to demonstrate how she'd tried to make friends with the bird. "But that bird, he no love me too much," she said, still laughing.

Angelo responded to Craig's puzzled look. "It was lipstick, all over my poor bird!"

I'd seen this over and over with Maria – her love could be hard to take. The turtle in our pond was becoming alarmingly reclusive because Maria liked to snag him every time she saw him and carry him around, poking at his little feet with her fingernail, exclaiming how cute he was and trying to coax him into sticking his head out. In April a guest had arrived with a guinea pig, which Maria pegged as a bunny with short ears. Craig and I watched on with alarm as Maria hugged (read: nearly strangled) the little black creature, both of us looking for telltale signs of suffocation while the blissfully unaware guests observed Maria indulgently.

But Smokey seemed able to take her love, and loved her back to distraction, even if he did occasionally have to protect himself.

So when Smokey, who by all estimates was roughly eighteen years old and only had one tooth left, started getting sick, Maria was distraught.

One day, at lunch over Nina's famous caesar salad, we had a long and serious talk with Maria trying to dissuade her from taking Smokey to the vet and putting him to sleep. For starters, there was the obvious problem that he was not our cat and our neighbors would not necessarily look fondly upon us stealing their cat and killing him. Secondly, I don't think anyone besides Maria had the heart to face the fact that Smokey was dying.

Not too many days later, Smokey finally passed away on Maria's day off, under our house.

At loose ends of how to deal with the dead body, the very questionable choice was made to put him in the garbage. Hindsight is 20/20, but foresight can often use some improvement. Sometimes drastically.

Someone forgot to take the garbage out.

There was some contention that Waste Management had refused to pick up garbage with a dead animal in it. How they would have known that the can contained Smokey is anybody's guess.

Regardless, Maria had noticed the garbage when she arrived the next morning. In hopes of getting it to the curb prior to the garbage men arriving (backed up garbage at a guesthouse is a nightmare even if there's not a dead animal involved), she'd tried to take it out. It was too late, but she noticed the smell. She opened the lid, saw the black bag and opened it. There lay her beloved cat.

Nina called Waste Management and (not mentioning the dead cat) managed to arrange for a pick up that afternoon. All morning, on the curb, like the coffin that it was, sat the disrespectful garbage can baking in the sun.

Here's to Smokey. Here's to Big. We're sorry that your end was not more dignified. But you were a beloved cat, perhaps mostly to Maria, but certainly to us all. Rest in peace.

Joe-Joe The One-Armed Painter

My husband wanted to paint the cottage. It was his contention that it looked like hell. And, admittedly, guests checking into Bamboo Hideaway or Gracie's Green Room cringed as I led them to their room. The paint on the siding was chipped and peeling, the windows were covered with rusty bars and the window trim had seen many years since it had last seen white. I wasn't positive we didn't have more pressing issues, but he was insistent. He was embarrassed.

So one morning in November, soon after Fantasy Fest, Craig took off for Sherwin Williams. He had a plan. He would use the sawzall to cut through and remove the bars, patch all holes, and then paint the cottage. The weather had finally cooled. It was perfect for outdoor work.

Maria was tickled. Every improvement we did to Orchids put her in a good mood for weeks. In some odd way, they justified her love of the neglected building.

"Soo-san," she told me breathlessly in the kitchen. "It will look beautiful." She sighed happily.

"Hmm..." I answered, eyeing the old-fashioned stove that exuded loads of character and had only one working burner. I wondered again about our priorities.

Craig arrived back at the guesthouse. We went out to greet him. Maria was nearly dancing in anticipation. But he wasn't alone. Craig grabbed four gallons of paint from the back of the truck. They hung from his hands like a promise of better things to come. Meanwhile, a man struggled to get out of the front seat.

The man was disheveled, in need of a haircut and a change of clothes. Even from a distance, he smelled. He reached into the car and grabbed a black garbage bag. I found out later that the bag held the needed change of clothes along with all of his other earthly possessions. Craig walked towards us, shoulders back, paint swinging, daring us to say anything. We didn't. We stood and stared.

"This is Joe-Joe," he introduced us. "He's going to help with the painting."

"Nice to meet you, Joe-Joe," I said after what was probably a rude pause. I reached out to shake his hand. He dropped the garbage bag and took my right hand in his left. About then I noticed he only had one arm.

"I sure could use a shower," he informed me wistfully.

"Umm..." I answered smartly.

"We've got work to do, Joe-Joe," Craig answered in lieu of an answer.

"Nice to meet you," Joe-Joe told me as he was led away.

"Who that?" Maria demanded as they rounded the house.

"I don't know," I responded truthfully.

"I no like," she told me.

"I'm sure he's very nice," I answered, not at all sure.

Later that day I cornered Craig. We were well out of hearing distance from both Maria and our new one-armed painter.

"Who is he?" I asked.

"He's a painter," Craig answered defensively.

"He's got one arm," I mentioned, in case he'd failed to notice.

"So?"

"How can he be a painter with only one arm?"

"It doesn't take two hands to hold a brush, Sue," he said scathingly.

"Okay." He had a point. "But where'd you get him?"

"He was outside the paint store."

"And?"

"He saw me buying paint, asked if I'd like some help."

"I suppose references would be out of the question?"

"He needs a break. And he said he had experience. What's the problem?"

Right. What was the problem? Apparently it was that I was shallower than I'd ever before suspected.

"What's in that bag he carries?"

"I think it's his stuff," Craig admitted, studying his shoes.

"His stuff?"

"Yeah. When I picked him up we had to go behind Albertson's. To get his stuff."

"What, like in the employee lounge?"

"No, like beside the dumpsters."

I nodded slowly, taking this in.

"Everyone needs a break, Sue," he reiterated stubbornly.

I kept nodding.

That evening, as the sun was setting, we were sitting at the back table having a glass of wine. It was almost time to go home for the day. Joe-Joe was still painting the back cottage. In the six hours since he'd started working, I calculated that he'd painted nearly half of one window. Wonderful.

"We should get going," I told Craig.

"Okay. But I have to give Joe-Joe a lift."

I pondered this for a moment. "To where?" I finally asked.

"Back to Albertson's, I guess," he answered with a shrug.

I sighed. "Fine."

"You got any cash on you?" he asked after a moment.

"Sure. There's some in the blue box. Why?" The blue box was kept in the employee bathroom. In it we kept cash from bicycle rentals, guests who paid cash, etc. It usually had a couple of hundred dollars.

"I have to pay him, Sue," he informed me, exasperated.

"Right."

Craig retrieved $60 from the box and retrieved Joe-Joe from the cottage. They made arrangements for the next day. Joe-Joe thanked me politely and said good-night. I was ashamed of myself.

The next morning I came outside for a cup of coffee after breakfast. Joe-Joe was steadily working on the same window. He was nearly finished, except that the top piece of trim was out of reach. He got a ladder and started to climb. I held my breath as he tried to balance with the paint can hanging off a hook at his waist (a hook that I later found out Craig had bought for him) and a paint brush in his only hand. He swayed backwards, caught himself, and continued upwards. The window got finished.

Joe-Joe stepped down off the ladder and stood back to admire his work. It did look nice. He noticed me at the table and smiled shyly. I smiled back and gave him a thumbs-up on the job. He took it as an invitation and meandered over.

"What do you think?" he asked, milking the moment.

"It's great," I replied. "It really makes a difference. I can't wait to see the whole thing done."

He grinned. "Do you mind if I grab a beer from your fridge?"

There were several reasons why, yes, I minded. In no particular order:

1.) It was 11 a.m.

2.) Even I wasn't drinking yet.

3.) At $10 an hour, I wasn't inclined to throw in free beers.

4.) I'd just witnessed his balancing act on a ladder and had no desire to increase the level of difficulty through alcohol.

"I do mind. Maybe at the end of the day."

He shot me a sullen look and headed back to painting. He worked the rest of the day. We didn't speak again.

The next morning Craig went to pick up Joe-Joe. Soon after he walked out the door, Joe-Joe called from a pay phone. The connection was not great.

"I'm gonna be late today!" he shouted.

"Craig's on his way to pick you up!" I shouted back.

"I'm not there!"

Craig returned to the guesthouse twenty minutes later. He was pissed. I told him about the phone call. Joe-Joe called back a couple of hours later, ready for his ride. Craig refused, angry. But nonetheless he agreed to give him a second chance and meet him the next morning at the scheduled time and place. Albertson's, by the dumpsters, I assumed.

The next morning Craig went to the meeting spot. He returned alone.

"No show?" I guessed smugly as he walked up the front steps.

"He was there. But he's decided to go back to Tampa. It's where he's from, and he's got family there. He's using the money he made for a bus ticket."

I thought about it. Thought about life by the Albertson's dumpsters. "Not a bad idea, probably."

Craig nodded. "Probably best. For him."

I figured it might be best for us as well, but said nothing.

Maria was happy Joe-Joe was gone. She'd never trusted him. Having been raised in a country where poverty, drugs and violence were an everyday part of life, she had black and white lines and made no apologies.

I, on the other hand, was raised with the luxury of guilt. And I couldn't help but admire my husband. Where I was talk, he was action. And because of him, hopefully, Joe-Joe was on a bus to a better place.

Animals

We have two dogs, Sneaker and Pokey. They've both strived for years to live up to their names and have admirably succeeded. Before we bought Orchids, they were used to us being around all the time. After the purchase, they saw us for an average of three hours a day, one in the morning and two at night before we passed out. It was no life for a dog.

We felt bad. Really bad. So we set out to correct the problem. The only solution was to integrate our dogs into life at the guesthouse.

We knew this would take some effort and it couldn't be done while we were working. So, for the love of our dogs, we decided to forfeit a day off.

We waited until late morning to avoid the breakfast crowd, and then walked Sneaker and Pokey the four blocks to the guesthouse. We told each other the exercise might make for a calmer introduction. I think we were secretly hoping they would pass out from exhaustion by the time we arrived. Unfortunately, our dogs are made of sterner stuff.

I'd made split pea soup to take with us so we could all have lunch together. Maria called it the Green Soup, and it was one of her favorites. I wouldn't have dared to turn up at Orchids around mealtime without food for the staff.

I had Pokey on her leash, Craig had Sneaker on his. Pokey and I were in the lead by quite a bit. At age 11 she's one year younger than Sneaker, and she's a tugger. We were always in the lead.

She barreled into the house as if she'd been going there daily. I can only figure she could smell us all over the place. I ran up the steps behind her.

Maria was in the hallway, talking to a guest in front of the open door to Fisherman's Retreat. She held something in her hand.

I was trying to get Pokey under control. She loved Maria, whom she'd met at our house on numerous occasions, and seemed to think she'd won the lottery to find her in this strange hallway.

"Is no people poo," Maria was saying to the large sweating woman in front of her.

"I think it might be," the guest insisted.

"No," Maria sniffed the paper towel in her hand. "It smell like tuna. Is cat poo."

She offered it to the guest, apparently suggesting the woman take a sniff. She declined.

I reined Pokey in and stood back. I didn't know what was going on, but felt confident this was not a conversation I wanted any part of. Out of the corner of my eye, I saw Craig taking Sneaker around the side to the back.

"Is too small for people poo," Maria continued assuredly, after studying the pile in the paper towel for a moment.

"You think?" the woman finally conceded.

"I sure. Fred. He did." She named her least favorite of our cats.

The guest nodded reluctantly. She shoved thick glasses up her nose and eyeballed Maria's handful of poo from a safe distance.

Pokey, who had been wriggling next to me with excitement, finally let out a yelp of hello to Maria. Both women turned towards me.

"Pokey!" Maria exclaimed in a high voice, kneeling on the floor and opening her arms. There was good reason the dogs loved her.

I undid Pokey's leash and she ran for Maria. They hugged and kissed each other.

"Hello, Cindy," I greeted the guest half-heartedly.

"Susan," she said breathlessly. "I think someone took a poo in front of my door last night."

Maria stood up with her hands on her hips, much to Pokey's disappointment.

"I tell her it no people poo," she said, shooting a dirty look at Cindy. "You want to smell?" she asked me, holding the paper towel in my direction.

"No. Thanks. I'm sure Maria's right," I told the guest. "I apologize. That's why we don't want the cats locked in the house at night. I am sorry." I gave her my best contrite expression.

I have to admit I found myself wondering what had happened in Cindy's life that led her to the automatic conclusion that a human had pooed on her doorstep. With four cats roaming the property, it seemed there were more obvious and simpler explanations.

"Pokey?" Maria called suddenly.

Good Lord, she was right. My dog had disappeared. We all looked around the hallway. My moment of panic passed when Pokey reappeared, out of Cindy's room.

"There you are!" I exclaimed, relieved. I clipped her leash back on.

Cindy reached down and patted Pokey's head. Three quick taps on the top of her skull. Pokey ducked away.

"Well, Cindy. Sorry again," I said, backing away and pulling my dog with me.

"No problem. As long as you're sure it was cat poo?" she answered.

"I'm positive." I smiled reassuringly.

She returned the smile, a little less than enthusiastically, and went back inside her room. Maria and I rolled our eyes at each other.

"I brought almuerzo," I whispered to her, using the Spanish word for lunch. "Are you almost done?"

"Si. Ten minutes."

"I'll get it ready." I smiled at her and squeezed her hand - the one that wasn't holding the poo.

We started to walk away when we heard Cindy squeal in her room.

The door flew open.

"Somebody has peed in my room," she sobbed.

Maria and I immediately looked at Pokey. She studied the baseboards and avoided our eyes.

"Somebody here hates me!" Cindy cried.

"No, Cindy, I'm so sorry. Again. It must have been Pokey," I said soothingly.

"Who?" she asked, hiccuping.

"My dog. Remember? She was in your room?"

She stared at me blankly.

"About three minutes ago," I added helpfully.

She nodded slowly. "So you think it was her?"

"Yes. I'm positive."

"You want I clean it up?" Maria offered considerately.

"I don't think that's necessary," I said quickly. Maria had done more than her fair share that morning. "It was definitely Pokey. She's overly excited. That's all."

Cindy stared at me, searching for weakness in my story. Finding none, she finally agreed.

I went for paper towels and some Clorox to clean up. I handed Pokey off to Craig who was sitting at the back table with Nina, waiting for lunch. He managed to look inconvenienced. I ignored him.

A half hour later the four of us were sitting at the table, enjoying soup and some fresh bread from Cole's Peace bakery. Maria and I hadn't had time to fill in Craig and Nina on the Cat Poo Incident.

Cindy walked out the back door. She was wearing a bathing suit and had wrapped a towel around her waist. The towel did little to save our appetites that were lost on the bathing suit. She smiled weakly at us and went down towards the pool.

Craig jumped up. "I should go skim the pool if she's getting in," he explained.

    The rest of us took no notice and kept eating. Craig returned several minutes later. He looked mystified.

    "Do you know what that woman just said to me?" he asked the table at large. We all shook our heads.

    "She said, 'I know it was human poo.'"

    Maria spit her soup out and cracked up. She slapped her knee. I couldn't help but giggle. Maria had this deep-in-her-belly kind of laugh that made it almost impossible to not laugh with her. Nina smiled vaguely.

    "What the hell does that mean?" Craig asked, still puzzled.

    Maria laughed even harder.

Diary of a Key West Innkeeper

Lunch

"Are you sure she's in there?"

"The key was gone from the lockbox."

When guests were arriving late at night, we left a Welcome Note on the door for them and put the key to their room in a lockbox beside the front door. The lockbox was a small locked metal box that needed a combination to open it. It was set to their zip code. It ensured safety for the house and sometimes a decent night's sleep for us.

"Maybe she went out early?" Nina suggested, staring at the door of Gracie's Green Room, one of our back cottage rooms with an outside private entrance. It was a cute room - small, cathedral ceiling, private bath. The only downside was its location directly off the deck where so many gatherings took place. Kind of like the one that was happening now.

It was three o'clock on a lazy summer afternoon and we were all sitting at the back table, finishing the jambalaya I had made the night before.

Nina, although not on shift, had come in to join us for lunch. I was learning quickly that free food was a job perk in Key West where normal benefits such as a health plan were rarely a consideration.

Nina had once mentioned that she would appreciate a dental plan in conjunction with her employment. After I stopped laughing, I looked at her teeth and asked her why. She was, after all, young and healthy and her teeth appeared straight and in good condition.

"I would like to get them whitened," she informed me.

I offered to buy her Crest Whitening Strips for Christmas.

"No, no. She no go," Maria disagreed with Nina's suggestion that Gracie's Green Room guest might have enjoyed an early outing. Maria got to the house around six most mornings. At least that's what she told us and we believed her. There was no reason to doubt as we had never, and would never, arrive early enough to check. Guests simply did not get up and leave before Maria arrived. It was unheard of.

We all nodded at this added piece of knowledge and stared at the door. Nina helped herself to another slice of bread. Craig sipped his wine. I lit a cigarette.

"I think she dead," Maria stated finally.

We stared some more.

"Maybe," I conceded.

"Perhaps she hung herself," Nina suggested, chewing thoughtfully.

"Nope. Overdose-ed. Drugs." Maria stated with confidence, pronouncing the 'ed' at the end of the word as an extra syllable. She stuck out her tongue and swung her head to the side, imitating a corpse.

"Maybe she had a heart attack," I said hopefully. For some reason, a death from natural causes seemed marginally better than a drug-induced suicide.

"Someone should find out," Craig said, his sunglasses low on his nose, his feet propped on the corner of the table as he tilted back in his chair.

"Nina, you should knock," I proposed.

"No way. I'm not even working."

"Maria?"

"No, no, no. I no do."

"Craig?"

"I'm resting."

Great. I stared at the door, willing our newest guest to pop it open and wish us all a hearty "Good afternoon!"

Didn't happen.

Nina started humming the radio jingle for Stellar Carpet under her breath. It was a catchy tune. If you live in Key West, you know the one I'm talking about. You're probably humming it right now.

"Who's that?" Craig asked, glancing across the backyard. We directed our attention to the couple who had just stepped into the Jacuzzi.

I studied them for a moment. "I don't know them. Nina?"

She stopped humming. "They don't look familiar."

"Maria?"

"I no think they stay here," she said after a moment. Two weeks earlier a nice man had approached Maria at the laundry machines and, very embarrassed, admitted that his wife had had too much to drink the night before and had thrown up all over the linens. He had them in a garbage bag and asked if she would mind washing them and giving him a replacement set. She'd agreed happily. Believe it or not, sheets could undergo far worse. When she asked his room number so she could bring him replacements, he told her 4C. That room did not exist in our hotel. Confused, she asked him to tell her where it was. He pointed to a balcony suite in the hotel next door.

So we were not completely unprepared for the occasional misdirected guest. The only difference was that the people now enjoying our Jacuzzi, as they didn't pass by our lunch table, had accessed our back yard by climbing the 3-foot coral wall that separated the two properties on that side. As a guest at a hotel, I think I would find the climbing of a rock wall an indicator that perhaps I was leaving the grounds or, at the very least, entering a section of the property that I was not invited to. But that's just me.

I walked towards the Jacuzzi, privately grateful to be avoiding the dead body in Gracie's Green Room, at least temporarily. Maybe Craig would be done with his 'rest' by the time I sorted this out.

"Hello!" I said to the couple, smiling broadly in case we were wrong and they did belong to us.

The man nodded shortly. The woman, head back, eyes closed, relaxing against the edge of the Jacuzzi, did not even look at me.

"I'm sorry to interrupt," I started.

"That's okay. Actually, we could use a couple of ice waters. Thanks." The woman did not open her eyes to utter her request.

For a moment, my natural urge to please made me consider getting them water and then determining if they were our guests. It was only the fact that I would have had to explain myself to Maria, Nina and Craig as I passed them that stopped me.

"Could I ask what room you're staying in?" I persisted.

"2B. Why? Do you charge for water?" the man answered testily.

His room number confirmed our suspicions. "No sir. But you are not at your hotel. Your hotel is over there."

Oh my God! She opened her eyes! "What?" she said.

"You are at the wrong hotel. And I'm sorry, we can't allow you to stay in the Jacuzzi." This last bit was probably unnecessary as he was already standing up. I was just feeling my authority.

"Well, where's our Jacuzzi?" he asked, looking at me expectantly.

"I'm not sure, sir. I'm not overly familiar with your grounds." This was true.

"We're supposed to have one."

How is this my problem? I thought. "I suggest you ask at your hotel."

"Fine." They got up and wrapped themselves in their towels. Nice towels. I wondered briefly if they'd brought them from up north or if our neighbors supplied that kind of quality.

The couple stalked off in a huff, as if I'd done something to offend them. I thought I was being quite generous to allow them to exit dripping through our house rather than insisting they go back through the bushes and over the fence.

    I returned to the table. My husband and staff had lost all interest in my little backyard scuffle and were once again staring at the door to Gracie's Green Room.

    "Before you sit down, Sue, knock on that door." Craig's feet were still resting on the corner of the table. By now he had lit a cigarette.

    "I suppose you're still resting?" I inquired with what I hoped was biting sarcasm.

    "Yep," he answered, oblivious. I'm often too subtle.

    To hell with it, I figured, and spun around to the door. I knocked ever so softly. The door flew open as if she'd been crouched on the other side. Waiting.

    "Miss Helman - I'm sorry to disturb you. We just wanted to make sure you were okay," I stammered.

    Wild red hair stood up in tufts all over her head. She wore a pink negligee that clung to her surprisingly well-preserved body. She glared at me.

    "Who are you?"

    "I'm the owner. Susan. I think we spoke on the phone when you made your reservation."

    "Hmph."

    "Again, I'm sorry. We just thought you might be dead." Of course I regretted the words as soon as they were out of my mouth. But, especially when nervous, I have a tendency to blurt out almost anything.

    "I'm not," she told me simply.

    "I see."

    "I'll be out in a little bit. Let me get dressed."

    "Sure. Sorry."

    I backed away from the door. She swung it almost shut, leaving a crack. I could see her eye through the shadows, watching me. I smiled brightly and turned to sit back down at the table.

    "Told you. Drugs," Maria said decisively and reached for Craig's wine to take a swig. She hated the stuff but forced a little down every day as she'd read a report that it was good for her heart.

    I rubbed my eyes. Nina resumed humming. Maria started picking up the lunch plates and Nina meandered inside to help clean up the kitchen. Craig rocked a little farther back in his chair, balancing his half-empty glass on his stomach. I found myself hoping he'd tip over.

He glanced at the door to Gracie's Green Room, which had finally closed completely, then looked back at me. He raised his eyebrows.

"What?" I asked.

"You made that reservation?"

"Yes. Obviously."

"Good one, Sue."

Diary of a Key West Innkeeper

New Friends

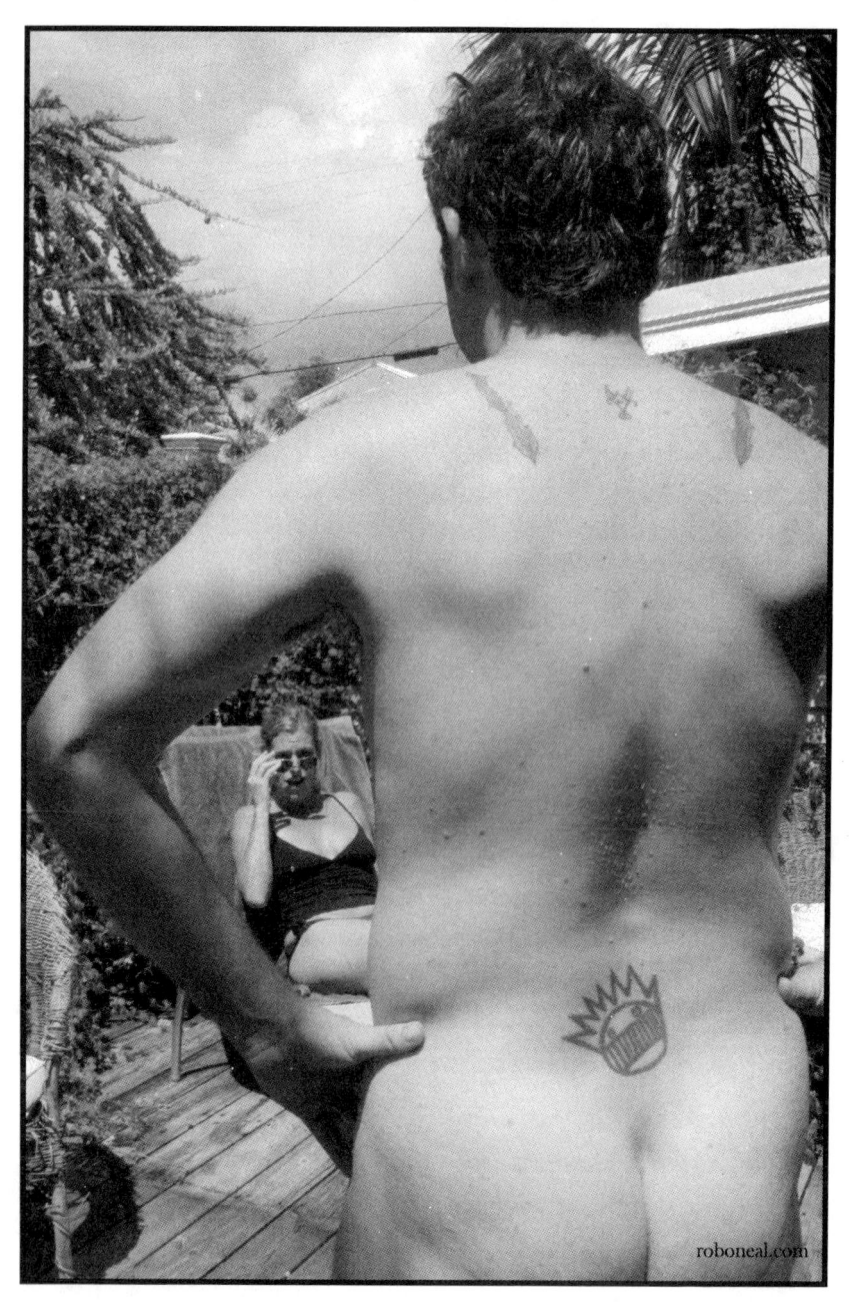

48

There was something growing on the side of my head. I noticed it when it was about the size of a peanut. It was now nearing the size of a walnut. I expected to wake up any morning to find that it had developed eyes and a mouth and started talking.

As it grew, I noticed that our guests stopped looking me in the eyes. I think they were afraid of their gaze sliding over to my second head. Perhaps they were even more afraid it would wink at them. I got a lot of comments on my outfits.

Craig, not nearly so shy, spent hours studying it and commenting.

"Jesus, Sue. You really need to get that thing taken off."

"I'm sure it will go away."

"Yeah? Cause I think it's gotten bigger since yesterday."

I reached up to feel it. He might have been right. Still, I was convinced that it might leave of its own volition, return to whatever world it had crawled out of.

One morning, Craig, me and the new friend on the side of my head, took off for the guesthouse.

I went to the computer, grateful that the growth was on my left side, and therefore didn't ruin any appetites as guests passed me on their way to breakfast. I could hear Craig and Maria chatting around the corner in the kitchen.

She was telling him a story in a stage whisper that was clearly audible throughout the first floor.

"He sit there, eating my beautiful breakfast. He has robe. Open! His thing...how you say?" I glanced into the open doorway and saw Maria pointing at Craig's groin area.

"His penis?" Craig guessed.

"Yes! Yes! His penis. It hang out!"

Craig laughed. So did I.

"I no look." Maria informed him primly.

"So how did you know?" he questioned, teasingly.

"I no look!" Maria insisted emphatically.

"If you no look, how do you know his penis was hanging out?" Craig continued.

Maria looked flustered.

"Was it big?" Craig asked her, mock serious.

"No," she answered solemnly. "Piquito...small!" She held her fingers up and indicated a length of about one inch. I was beyond-words grateful that the French man was nowhere in hearing distance.

"You were looking!" Craig shouted, joking with her.

She scowled at him and went back to her pancakes. "I no look," she muttered.

The guest to whom she referred was visiting from France with his wife. They were in their mid-fifties and obviously not as squeamish about the human body as Americans tended to be. They were trying to teach us French customs, and we were enjoying learning them. However, while we were amenable to shaking hands every morning, I was thinking Craig would probably stop short of bearing his privates at the breakfast table.

Luckily, our French friends ate very early, before any other guests were up and about. Plus, they were checking out the following day. We figured ultimately it didn't need addressing.

Our new mantra at the guesthouse was something along the lines of, "Why deal with that which you can ignore?" It was working fairly well.

Later that afternoon I was sitting outside with Beverly Helman. After a rocky start of wagering on the likelihood of her surviving her first night, we had come to love her. She encouraged mimosa mornings and wine-filled afternoons. Bev and I were joined by another guest, Stan. He came in to town and stayed with us so often he was like family. He was a good-looking man in his mid-thirties who told us silly jokes and brought valentines for the whole staff (except Craig) in February. Bev and I were sipping a glass of wine. Stan abstained, which was his habit. We were chatting about nothing in particular.

"So," Stan said after a comfortable pause in the conversation. "I don't mean to pry, Sue, but what the hell is that thing on the side of your head?"

"Yeah," Bev added casually. "I have been wondering about that."

I blushed deep red and my hand flew to the side of my head, trying to cover the new addition.

"I don't know," I admitted finally.

"You should get that checked out," Bev told me serenely. "It could be cancer."

Stan nodded his agreement.

Right then, thankfully, the wife of our French Flasher sauntered out of the back cottage, in plain view of our gathering. She was naked, carrying a towel. She waved at us. Mouths agape, we waved back. She stepped carefully into the pool, testing the temperature. Apparently pleased, she sank into the water up to her neck. We continued to stare at her bobbing head.

None of us heard my husband joining us at the table until he pulled a chair out. He poured a glass of wine. I think we looked guilty.

"What's going on?" he questioned, lighting a cigarette. Bev helped herself to one and Craig lit it for her.

"The French lady is naked in the pool," I whispered, in roughly the same stage whisper Maria had used that morning.

"Oh," Craig answered, frowning.

"What should we do?" I asked.

"Maybe you should go tell her that we are not clothing optional," he suggested logically.

"Maybe you should," I shot back.

"I'm not going up to a naked lady and having a conversation," he countered. Bev and Stan watched our conversation with interest, like people following a ping-pong match.

"No one else is here," I suggested hesitantly.

My husband saw where I was going with this. "You sure?"

"Yeah," I answered, gaining confidence. "The rest of the house is out."

"Well," he agreed, "If she gets out before anyone else comes home..."

The table nodded solemnly. No need to unduly embarrass a 50-year-old French lady. We all waited, subdued, one eye on the front door, one eye on the pool. Finally, she emerged. And, with another wave to our group, she headed back into the cottage. We exhaled collectively in relief.

Bev sipped her wine. "So, about this thing on your head," she resumed.

"I'll go to a doctor," I agreed, resigned.

(Note: The growth on the side of my face was a subcutaneous cyst. It was successfully and painfully removed two hours later at the local clinic. It required three stitches to close the incision. It was not malignant.)

Diary of a Key West Innkeeper

I made a fountain

52

I made a fountain

We woke up to the sound of the phone ringing. It was early on Christmas morning, our first Christmas since buying the guesthouse. The call went to voicemail as we lay in the bed, staring silently at the ceiling and praying for a wrong number or a friend in a foreign country miscalculating the time change. Maria was working that morning at Orchids. We'd offered her the day off, due to the holiday, but her Navy husband was stationed overseas and her son was also out of town. She said she'd rather spend Christmas at the guesthouse than alone.

Almost immediately, the ringing started again. Craig cursed and threw the covers off. He dashed for the living room. I listened from the bed, barely breathing, afraid of missing a word.

"Hola, Maria! Feliz Navidad!" He forced good cheer into his voice, although I know he realized, as did I, that a 7 a.m. phone call from Maria could mean nothing good.

He recounted the conversation for me after they'd hung up – while he and I were throwing our clothes on.

"Hello, Greg," Maria answered him in a breathless voice. She slowed down. "How are you?" she asked, unerringly polite as was her habit.

"I'm good, Maria, how are you?" he answered, speaking clearly and deliberately as was our habit with Maria.

"I made a fountain!" Maria exclaimed, still trying to catch her breath.

"Wow! That's wonderful!" My husband replied, actually deluding himself for a moment that Maria had called and dragged us out of bed to announce an early Christmas present.

"No, no, no," she continued impatiently, "A fountain in the backyard."

"It sounds nice – I can't wait to see it." I had managed to get out of bed and was now standing anxiously in the doorway, listening to the call. I could hear the smile in Craig's voice as he spoke indulgently into the phone. All was well.

"No!" Maria shouted in frustration, I could actually hear her from where I stood. "A fountain all over the backyard. Water all over."

Craig paused, thinking hard. After all, he had just woken up. "A flood?" he asked, comprehension dawning.

"Si! Si! A flood!" Maria exclaimed, relieved.
"How?"
"It was the pipe. She broke. You come now."
He hung up the phone.

I had moved into the hallway and was squinting in his general direction. I hadn't had time to find my glasses.

"What's up?"

"I think a pipe broke off. I think something is flooding."

"Great," I said, moving towards the bedroom to get dressed. Craig followed.

We pulled on some clothes. Craig ran the dogs outside for a quick walk while I got their breakfast ready. Seven minutes after the phone call we were walking out the front door with our dogs glancing up, puzzled, as they ate.

Craig pulled the door shut behind us. "Merry fucking Christmas," he muttered to my back as we headed for the scooter.

"Merry Christmas," I agreed softly.

No guests were yet awake when we arrived. But Maria was a flurry of frantic activity - accomplishing nothing. Mostly because there was nothing to accomplish.

She told us what had happened in quick, broken English.

"I do happy Christmas for you. Clean pools. I no like water, but I want for you. So I start and she break off and water everywhere!" She was near tears.

We pieced the situation together quickly.

Maria, who refused to clean the pools because she couldn't swim and was afraid of water, had decided to surprise us for Christmas. She'd swallowed her fear and took it upon herself to do this one chore for us on Christmas morning. Pulling the hose, which could be very stubborn, over to the big pool, she'd tugged too hard. The pipe had broken off at its base. And a fountain was born. Water gurgled merrily from the broken base, turning the back area around the breakfast tables into a wading pool. All that was missing was a toddler sitting in the center taking a pee.

We watched it silently.

After a moment, I spoke. "We need to cut the water to the house."

Craig thought about it. "We can't. People need to shower, flush the toilet. Plus we still need to get breakfast ready."

Maria fretted in Spanish beside us. The word "estupido" came up more than once.

Craig turned his attention to her. "This is not your fault," he said slowly, making sure she understood. "My fault. You understand?"

She nodded, unconvinced, and looked at me.

"He's right," I agreed. "Greg's fault. Greg's fault. Not you!"

Craig glared at me. "What are you, incapable of fixing something around here?"

I smiled sweetly at him. "It wasn't on my list. It was on yours." He scowled.

Maria stared at us suspiciously.

"Te quiero me amiga," I said to her in my limited Spanish. I hoped it translated in to "I love you my friend." I wasn't sure, but that's what I was shooting for.

I wasn't lying. It was Craig's fault. We'd known the pipe was not anchored properly to the house. Every day when Craig cleaned the pools he handled it with the utmost care. Tenderly. Fixing the pipe was on a long list of "to-do's" that had yet to be done. A list that seemed to grow daily. Maria couldn't have known this. She was just trying to give us a nice surprise.

"See if you can reach Frank," he said to me.

I nodded and walked listlessly towards the office. Frank was our plumber. A man that we thanked God for around the guesthouse on a nearly daily basis. But I was not optimistic about my odds of reaching him on Christmas day.

I dialed his number. I knew it by heart. "Merry Christmas!" I started to the answering machine, forcing a perky tone. Maybe I figured he'd be more inclined to interrupt Christmas with the family if we sounded like a fun place to be. "I'm so sorry to bother you. I don't know if there is any way you can come to Orchids today. I know it's a long shot...but we have a broken pipe in the backyard. And we can't cut the water. I'm so sorry, I don't know if you'll get this message, but..."

Frank's wife picked up the phone. Her warm friendly voice carried across the lines like a tonic. I almost sobbed in relief.

"Merry Christmas, Sue!" she said.

"It's Christmas," I agreed wryly.

"What happened?"

"I'm so sorry to bother you guys..."

"It's okay. Frank wasn't going to work today, but when I heard your voice I decided to pick up."

How did we get so lucky? I wondered briefly. It had recently occurred to us that we had done something terrible, perhaps in a past life, to anger the gods thus bringing the equivalent of the seven plagues of Egypt into our guesthouse. Yet here was evidence that we had at some point done something right, and paid proper homage to the God of

Plumbing Disasters. What a break! Do you have a better explanation for the ability to reach your plumber on Christmas morning?

I told her what had happened.

"Well, we've got to open gifts with the grandkids this morning. But we should be done around noon. How 'bout he comes out then and takes a look?"

"I think I love you," I exclaimed.

She chuckled. "I know you do. But maybe not quite so much after you get the bill."

She was wrong. The bill was more than fair. And I did love them. So much I started planning extravagant gifts to send. But, the road to hell is paved with good intentions, and I'm the queen of that. Shame on me, nothing ever made it into the mail except for the check that paid the bill.

Breakfast got started. The Thompsons were the first ones awake. Maria was still a bit flustered, but nonetheless cooked a beautiful breakfast. Craig and I stationed ourselves close to the kitchen to wish our guests a Merry Christmas and then try to explain the tsunami around the breakfast tables in a non-alarmist, casual sort of way.

The guests took it well, and a pile of shoes formed at the backdoor so they could wade to their tables without damaging their footware. They even laughed. It's possible that the mimosas we quickly assembled and served went a long way to smooth over the disaster. At any rate, they cheered me up.

My shoes joined the pile as I carried a bottle of champagne and a pitcher of orange juice out to the tables to refill everyone's cocktail. Some guests sat with their feet tucked up underneath them or propped on an opposing chair. The tipsier guests had their feet in the water. Small currents swirled around their ankles. I was certain it was not a Christmas breakfast that any would soon forget and sadly acknowledged to myself that we were not cultivating repeat guests that day. Amazingly, I was wrong about that.

Just before noon, ahead of schedule, Frank showed up. He had one of his sons, who helped with the business, in tow. I stopped just short of sinking to my knees and genuflecting.

They were going to have to cut the water to the house to repair the pipe.

Craig popped another bottle of champagne and went outside to announce this latest inconvenience to our assembly of guests paying high-season rates. Surprisingly, they were still all assembled at the breakfast tables. It was always shocking to me what people would put up with given

I made a fountain

free booze and good company. The flood eddied around them as they nodded complacently.

Frank cut the water and started to work on the pipe. At the table nearest to where he worked sat a retired plumbing supply salesman. The man was a little past buzzed and feeling inexplicably paternal towards my husband and myself. He'd decided that Frank was possibly suspect.

"Wha'cha doin' there, buddy?" he asked Frank, staring hard at his back.

Frank hitched up his pants, strapped on his knee pads and ignored him.

"Wha'cha usin' there, friend?" he persisted a bit louder.

Frank moved on deliberately, not even acknowledging the man's existence.

Craig grasped the situation and stepped in.

"Hey Billy," he walked up to the table. "Can you help me out for a sec?" The guest nodded slowly, reluctant to take his eyes of our plumber.

Craig led him away. I approached Frank. "You want a mimosa?" I asked him in lieu of an apology. Billy's family was still seated just feet away.

Frank gave me a characteristic crooked grin. "I'd rather have a beer."

I nodded and took off for the refrigerator. The man could have requested anything. I would have done it. This was easy. When I returned, he was removing his knee pads and instructing his son to turn the water back on. It was over. I handed him the beer and he nodded at me.

"Thank you," I said simply. Although not usually at a loss for words, nothing else seemed to do justice to my feelings at that moment.

"Anytime, Sue." He toasted me with his beer and took a long swallow.

Right then, I knew that he and I had a moment of pure understanding. He knew my plight. And I also knew that for whatever the reasons, we could count on the God of Plumbing Disasters to smile on us again in the future. Unfortunately, it would be the very near future.

Or maybe we were just luckier than we thought, because at least we had Frank.

And we had Maria, who cared enough to try to give us a Christmas present.

Diary of a Key West Innkeeper

A Good Night's Sleep

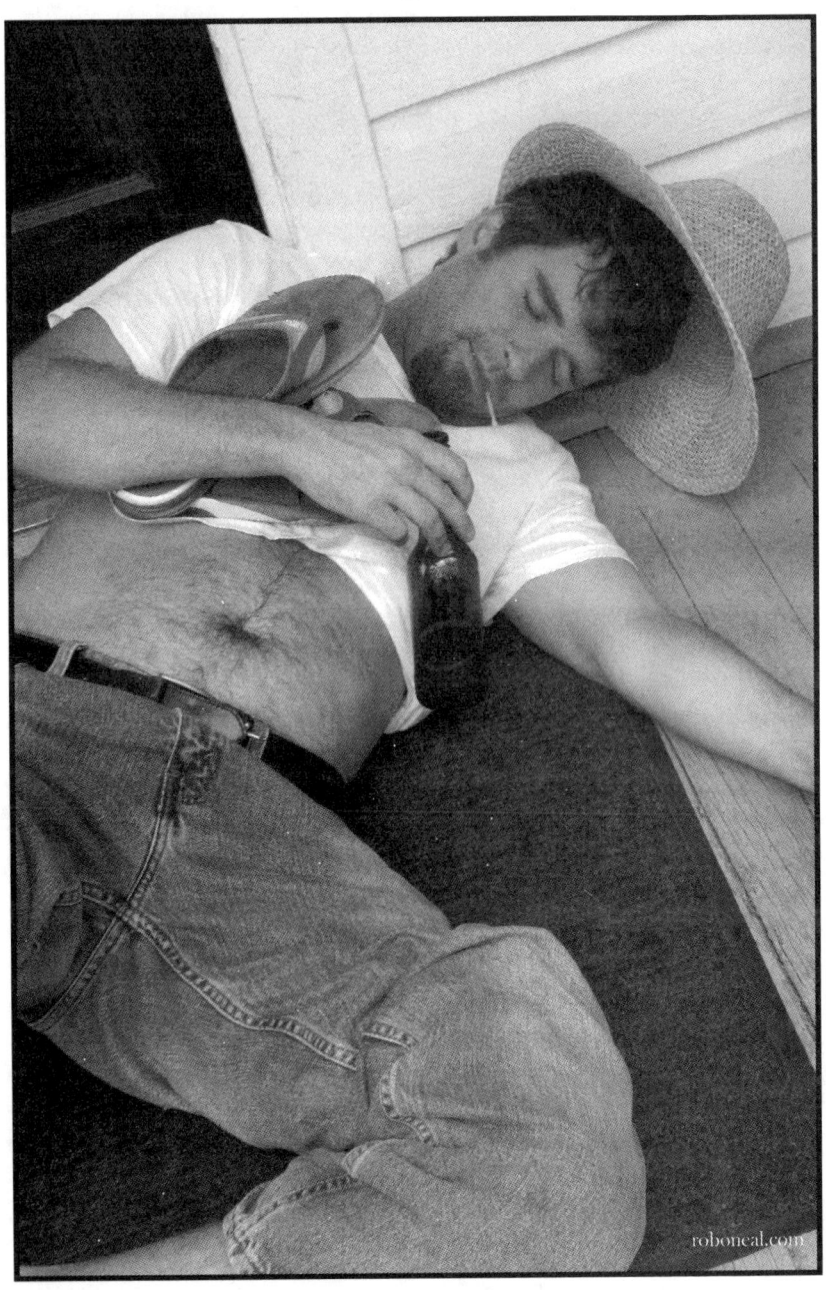

It was 64 degrees.

I know, I know. You people up North are thinking, "Hey, that's downright balmy." But it's not. Not when your blood has adjusted to constant temperatures above 85. In that case, it's downright freezing. Might as well snow.

So, as all residents of the southernmost town are obligated to do at least a couple of times during the winter, we dug through the odd outdated assortment of clothing we had brought when we moved and tried to make an outfit. I wore long johns underneath a long flowered tropical skirt, white socks and black Birkenstocks, a cream fleece hat with a ball on top and a bulky sweater with three T-shirts underneath. For good measure (and because I was still cold) I wrapped a beach towel around my waist.

Guests, whose blood was obviously thicker, laughed. But they wouldn't be laughing for long. Temperatures were dipping into the 50's that night, and the guesthouse was equipped with neither down comforters nor heat.

We realized the problem before they did. And, as always when faced with a new dilemma, we sought out Maria.

"We put blankets and heaters," she told us confidently.

"Heaters?"

"Little heaters. For rooms." Space heaters! Brilliant.

Thank God there was a solution.

She showed my husband where the heaters were stored - a hidden shelf in the employee bathroom that could be reached only by dangling off the top of the toilet.

Maria and I went to the rooms to remake the beds with extra blankets as I gave one last concerned look over my shoulder at Craig balancing precariously while stretching for the hidden space heaters. Health insurance was well beyond our budget and I couldn't help but speculate as to the cost of a broken leg.

The blankets had been stored in the rooms in hidden drawers and chests I'd assumed were empty. They were blankets of the sort you would hope to never discover, much less suggest people paying over $200 per night should wrap themsleves in.

The first blanket we unearthed was in Bamboo Hideaway. It was poo-brown and fuzzy. 100 percent polyester, the label bragged. I was reminded of childhood Thanksgiving trips sleeping on my Grandmother's pull-out sofa in her tiny cottage in Tennessee. Unfortunately, the smell coming from the blankets was not nearly as

pleasant as Grandma's sweet potato casserole with marshmallows on top.
$215 a night. Great.

We moved on. In the Hibiscus Room, a dingy yellow blanket with conspicuous rust brown stains (that wouldn't be blood, would it?) emerged from a hidden drawer under the armoire.

The blankets continued to appear, with no notable improvements. The whole exercise was a disheartening task that finally ended with all of the beds remade in extra blankets that were probably older than me and were definitely the worse for wear.

Maria whistled cheerfully as we worked. The cool air was a godsend for housekeeping.

After we finished, I went to find my husband. He had unloaded the room heaters and lined them in the hallway.

"God," I started, "You should see these blankets. We have to order new ones."

He looked at me. "Can you count?"

I pondered for a moment, sure it was a trick question. "Yes," I finally conceded.

"Count the heaters."

I did. There were six. We had eight rooms.

"Wow. Someone's gonna be cold?" I suggested.

He didn't laugh.

"I've got to go to Kmart. I'll be back."

Right about here, we should have realized there was a reason to have only six heaters. But we didn't. We had admitted, if only amongst ourselves, that although we disagreed with the previous owner on many points there was occasionally some method to his madness. So maybe, just maybe, we should have thought about it a little further. Whatever.

Craig arrived back with the heaters and they joined the embarrassing blankets in every room. We left for the day confident that all of the guests would be warm and toasty for the upcoming chilly night. We were even a bit pleased with ourselves for our foresight. We made turkey sandwiches for dinner, walked the dogs and dozed off on the couch in front of "Law and Order." We stumbled into bed just before nine.

The phone started ringing at 12:20 a.m. I rolled out of bed, knocking my forehead hard on one of the posts of our bed. That was going to leave a mark.

I found the phone. Caller ID told me it was the emergency line we had installed at the front door of the guesthouse.

" 'Ello?" I croaked.

"Is Susan or Craig available?" Whoever it was, was wide awake.

"This is she."

"Sorry to bother you," he started, not actually sounding sorry at all. "But we're staying here at your guesthouse and we have no power."

"No power?"

"No. None."

"We'll be right there."

I stumbled back into the bedroom where Craig was already up and pulling blue-jeans over his long underwear. I started to do the same. It was like living in a firehouse, except instead of an impressive big red truck with sirens and flashing lights, we drove off on a little red scooter. Nonetheless, our response time was roughly three minutes.

Even considering the speed with which we dressed, the phone rang again before we got out the door.

"Yeah?" Craig answered shortly, assuming the same guest was calling back after an impatient wait of about 90 seconds.

Unfortunately, such was not our luck. It was a different guest. They had no power either. He assured them we were on our way and we started again for the door.

The phone rang. We looked at it for only a second and kept walking.

We scooted to the guesthouse and immediately noticed the landscaping and front porch lights that should have been on all night were off. Not a good sign.

A small gathering of people, maybe five or six, was milling around the darkened porch. Another couple was in the hallway. Craig went immediately to the breaker box at the side of the house. Not wanting to be obligated to give lunch suggestions for the next day to the growing crowd, I followed him. He started flipping breakers. A hopeful moment or two passed before they started flipping back.

"Shit," he muttered.

"Maybe we should stick a penny in them?" I suggested in a quiet voice from his shoulder.

He glanced back at me and narrowed his eyes. "I hope you're kidding."

I thought about it. I was sure I'd heard that worked.

"No, seriously."

"Unless you've reconsidered the idea of burning this place down, it's not a good idea, Sue."

"Oh."

"It's the damn heaters," he said, not really talking to me but I figured I'd talk back anyway.

"How? They've been used before, I'm sure."

"That's why there were only six." I could hear his teeth grinding.

"Well that's bullshit. What are we supposed to do, have them draw straws for heat?" I indicated the porch contingent that were chatting amongst themselves while trying to act like they weren't watching us.

"No. We have to move the heaters around the rooms. Put them in different plugs."

"How do you know which plugs they should go into?"

He was glaring. "I don't, Sue. If I did, I would have put them there to start."

"Oh."

"We have to move them around, trial and error. Do you understand?" He was speaking in tight measured tones, breathing hard.

"Don't get mad at me."

"You're the one who wanted a guesthouse." He stalked towards the front porch.

He explained the plan to the waiting guests. As they were on vacation and had just gotten in for the evening (thus all the heaters going on at once) nobody was overly inconvenienced. Nor, considering they were in a guesthouse with dubious power, overly alarmed. Bottom line, they took it well and inside of an hour we had the power redistributed.

We drove home silently. Craig sat on the couch, pissed, and puffed on a cigarette. I went to bed. He came in shortly after, rolling away from me and constructing a pillow barrier between us. I felt I was taking a little more blame than was my due, but was too tired to care. I went to sleep.

The phone rang at 5:05 a.m.

I rolled out of bed (again), but managed to miss hitting my throbbing forehead against the post (again). Caller ID told me it was the emergency phone at the front door of the guesthouse (again!).

" 'Lo?" I answered.

"Let me in," slurred a blatantly drunk man on the opposite end of the line.

I sighed. The sky was the tiniest bit grey from the upcoming dawn. "What room are you in?"

"Dunno," his voice grew faint, as if he were wandering off.

"Sir, are you sure you're staying with us?"

Craig appeared in the hallway, looking hostile.

"Yeah...this looks like the place."

"What is your name?"

"Hmm?"

"Your name, sir. What is your name?"

"Holloway."

I cursed myself for not having the laptop at home. That was, after all, one of the purposes behind buying it. I was 90 percent sure that no Holloways were staying with us. But 90 percent wasn't enough.

"I'll be there in just a minute."

"Yeah..." his voice was fading. He hung up.

"I'll go. You stay," I offered.

"Is he even our guest?"

I shrugged.

"Look him up on the computer."

"I can't. I left it there last night."

He snorted and looked off into space, as if trying to find the patience to deal with my inadequacies.

"I have to go."

Big sigh.

"I'll give you a lift." I glowed. After all these years, he still loved me.

We arrived at the guesthouse for the second time in six hours (all of them dark). We noted, gratefully, that the lights were on in front. A fat man with a stubbed out cigar and an oversized soda from the local Circle K was sleeping peacefully on a porch chair. He was not our guest.

Craig nudged him with his foot.

"Wrong house, buddy."

"Huh?"

"You are at the wrong hotel," I tried to explain.

"This looks like it," he told us.

"Well, it's not," Craig chimed back in.

"Do you know the name of your hotel?" I asked, hoping to help. It was, after all, very cold out.

He shook his head sadly as his eyes started to close.

"Well," said my husband, nudging him again with his foot, "You can't stay here. And we can't help you if you don't know where you're going. Move along."

The man staggered to his feet, steadying himself against the porch rail.

"Allright already," he slurred.

Craig helped him as he climbed down the porch stairs - we weren't completely without compassion. And, to be honest, a fat-man-tumble down the front steps was the last thing we needed that night. We watched him weave away on the sidewalk, studying the next guesthouse carefully as he passed. Two doors up the street, he turned and climbed onto their porch. Whether or not that's where he was actually staying or if he had just spotted a comfy-looking chair, hard to say.

The sun was rising. It was Maria's day off so we had to start work in an hour or so. There was little point in going back home. Even our dogs would not wake up for hours, and Craig could scoot home then to walk and feed them. As the greys of dawn faded into the colors of daylight, we made a pot of strong coffee and sat in the garden, not speaking. It was the beginning of another glorious day in Paradise.

Any Assistance is Appreciated

It was a sunny day in September, muggy and hot. I was sweating as I answered emails, wiping my face with a paper towel to keep from dripping on the keyboard and shorting it out. It was just after 9 a.m. A mosquito was loose under my desk and I was swinging my legs vigorously to try to discourage another bite. I couldn't catch her yet (not from a lack of effort), but I was confident that would soon change. Fat and full of my blood, eventually she'd make easy pickings. I looked forward to it with sweet anticipation. Of course, I'd probably have to sacrifice another pint or two first.

"Hello?" our friend, the manager of a neighboring guesthouse, called down the hall. Stella had a strong English accent that to me, regardless of any evidence to the contrary, always implied class and intelligence.

"Hey," I answered, turning away from the computer. I scratched my leg.

"How's it going?" she asked solicitously. The first couple of weeks she'd spent laughing at us. Apparently, our fantasy world of guesthouse ownership was just about the funniest thing she'd ever heard. But just recently that had segued into what appeared to be genuine concern. Perhaps it was our dead eyes and vacant stares.

I shrugged, despondent.

"It'll get better," she suggested with no real conviction.

"Sure..."

She sipped the cup of coffee that she'd brought along for the walk. I could tell she was stalling.

"What's up?" I finally asked.

"Well, you know Fantasy Fest is coming." Sure, the big festival of Key West, similar to Mardi Gras in New Orleans. Even I knew it was just around the corner.

"Each year one of the guesthouses on the block hosts a stop for the Locals' Parade," she continued.

"Okay..." Amazingly, I didn't see where she was headed.

"Sorry, Sue. This year is your year." Was she smirking? Or was I imagining that?

"What is it?"

She couldn't suppress a chuckle. She had been smirking!

"Well, about two thousand drunk locals in costumes walk around town and stop at various businesses for cocktails."

I stared at her. Surely she was kidding. "Two thousand?"

"Roughly."

"And we're supposed to serve them all drinks?"
"That's the gist of it."
"At the same time?"
"Yep."
"You're joking."
"You wish."

I considered refusing. Then I considered crying. Then, a thought occurred to me and a benign smile spread across my face.

"No problem," I agreed. Stella looked skeptical. But I'd realized something important. The parade was still five weeks away. And, let's be honest, nobody actually anticipated surviving that long. I put it completely out of my head.

Nearly a month passed in a haze of overflowing toilets, roof leaks, a broken dishwasher, a broken dryer, a broken pipe that knocked out the landscaping irrigation system, late nights trying to fill empty rooms, early mornings cooking breakfast and, of course, days and days of folding laundry. One week prior to the parade a bubbly woman with bleached hair, a permanent tan and perfect teeth that defied her age stopped by the house to drop off official bright red signs that said Locals' Parade Stop. She told me they should be prominently displayed. I smiled and thanked her and pretended that I knew what she was talking about. After she left, I eyeballed the signs stacked neatly on a kitchen chair. Something about the term Locals' Parade seemed vaguely familiar. In a sudden moment of insight, like a breakthrough with the psychiatrist I was considering hiring, the memory of Stella's visit returned to me.

I allowed a moment of pure panic to pass. What the hell, I figured after regaining my composure, maybe it would be fun?

We obviously needed more information. I located my husband scrubbing down a shower stall in an upstairs room and handed him the phone, understanding fully that it was an empty gesture as he had thus far refused to answer it. Our next door neighbor had hosted last year, and they therefore seemed like the right place to start.

After a little searching and a couple of wrong turns along their beautifully landscaped brick pathways, I found the office, marked by a cute old-fashioned wooden sign. I opened the door and was greeted with a blast of cold air. It was like visiting a foreign land. One I didn't want to leave.

Jen was at the desk. I couldn't help but notice that her perfectly pressed linen sun-dress was conspicuously lacking armpit sweat stains.

We exchanged quick greetings and I got down to business.

"Do you know what's up with this Locals' Parade thing?"

"I know I'm glad it's not our turn for another two years." She laughed.

"Is it that bad?"

I don't know if it was the tears welling in my eyes, or simply her basically good nature, but she stopped laughing and took pity.

"It's not that bad, Susan."

I sniffled.

"Look, I'll give you the recipe for the drinks we made last year. You buy thirty jugs of water and a clean garbage can, dump out the water, mix the cocktails in the garbage can and refill the jugs. Get ice and plastic cups from Waterfront Market and borrow some tables. It's not that big a deal."

No big deal. Sure. She had a staff of eight. I had a staff of one. And she was on vacation.

"Thank you," I offered meekly.

"Kevin and I can help, too. If you guys do one table, we'll man the other." She was a saint. I was embarrassed by my moments earlier urge to kill her.

"You guys are the best." Two months prior I was the kind of person who didn't like accepting help from anyone, no less someone I barely knew. These days I was mildly surprised that I didn't spend my days on my knees begging for assistance.

I returned to our guesthouse and answered the four calls that had gone to voice-mail in my absence. My husband had performed exactly as predicted. We had one last check-in before we were done for the day. The house was full, thanks to the upcoming Fantasy Fest, and would be for nine days. Translation: no rooms to turn over. It felt almost like vacation. And with the parade thing now well in hand, I was practically glowing.

Craig and I met at the back table for a glass of wine. There were only two loads of laundry left, breakfast was prepped, housekeeping was done and there was nothing to do but wait for the new arrivals.

"You got this parade-thing figured out?"

"Yep. No problem. I'll give you a list to pick up on Monday with the other groceries. Kevin and Jen are going to help."

"Who?"

"The guys from next door."

"Oh."

"Yep." We sipped our wine and I waited patiently. I could tell he was stewing.

"So what then?" he finally said. "We owe them a favor?" My husband hated owing anybody anything. He didn't quite yet share my change of heart on this subject. Give him time.

"Yes. We owe them a favor."

"I don't know if I like that." He stared at me through his sunglasses. Although I couldn't see his eyes, I was sure he was squinting suspiciously.

I thought about it. Took another sip. "I don't care."

He thought about it. Nodded. We were way too tired to fight each other. After all, as far as we could tell, the whole world was out to get us.

"Hello?" The voice came from the hallway.

I jumped up. "Hello!" I shouted in response.

Our final arrivals for the week had paid their taxi and made their way into the house. We checked them in and took off for the night.

The morning of the dreaded Locals' Parade finally arrived. My smug confidence had eroded the day before when Craig saw the shopping list.

"Where the fuck am I supposed to put thirty jugs of water? I'm going to have to make a separate trip." Sorry.

"Do you know how much this liquor is going to cost?" No, not really.

"Where are you getting the tables?" Actually, had forgotten that part.

"Have you arranged the ice?" No, but I have a plan.

"Two thousand plastic cups? Are you out of your mind?" Maybe.

The supplies were finally laid in, but Craig was not happy. Hell, nobody was.

That morning we arrived during breakfast. Thank God, Maria had come back from vacation and I was spared my morning ritual of sweating into the pancakes. I turned on the computer and said hello to a couple of guests. Craig stalked by the desk.

"What's wrong?" I asked, for what should be obvious reasons, dreading the answer.

"The Jacuzzi." He stared at a spot over my head.

"What's wrong with it?"

"Jesus, Sue. If I knew, we wouldn't be having this conversation. I have no idea. Come look."

I pointed someone in the direction of the coffee and followed him outside. The water in the Jacuzzi, which on its best day was a struggle to keep looking good, was covered in a thick mysterious brown scum. It looked like a huge vat of Guinness - dark and foamy. It occurred to me that we had guests who might consider drinking it. We stood and stared. Maria walked by briskly with an armful of plates from the breakfast tables.

"Is body paint," she informed us casually, never breaking stride.

"Is what?" I asked.

She stopped. "Body paint. Body paint," she repeated impatiently. "Dirty woman wash in Jacuzzi. Paint. You understand?"

I nodded slowly. I understood her words but was having trouble with their meaning. Body paint was a big deal at Fantasy Fest. Lots of people did it. And apparently, if Maria was correct, which she usually was, one of them had seen fit to bathe in our Jacuzzi.

"What do we do about it?"

She shrugged. "I no know." She walked off, whistling hello to our bird, Rocky. It was nice that she was happy to be back.

"We'll have to drain it," Craig announced after a moment, his shoulders slumped in defeat..

"Couldn't we try to chlorinate it?" I suggested, watching as dirty bubbles floated lazily through the sludge.

He sighed, already exhausted before 9:30am. "It won't work."

"I guess we should drain it," I conceded finally, after a couple minutes of silent contemplation. I was using the term "we" very loosely.

I knew I would not have anything to do with it. I had 2,000 cocktails to make.

"Where will the water go?" I asked tentatively.

He glared at me. But this was important! The Jacuzzi bordered the neighbor's property, right on the line. I was afraid that Jen and Kevin might be less amenable to helping me at the parade if we'd just dumped 250 gallons of toxic waste on their land.

"I don't know, Sue. I'll figure it out," he finally stated flatly.

"Try not to..." I faded off under the heat of his stare. Maybe they wouldn't notice until tomorrow. Maybe he could find another place for the water. Maybe a giant meteor would put us out of our misery.

Two hours later, the water was gone. I didn't ask where. Craig had just finished bleaching the Jacuzzi and it was slowly refilling. He mixed a Bloody Mary and lit a cigarette. Without a word or an offer to share, he took a seat at the back table. His expression was blank behind his sunglasses. I had gotten through my normal morning tasks and managed to borrow the tables for later. The ice was due to be delivered one hour before the parade. It was time to mix 2,000 drinks.

Craig dragged himself from the chair and we started hauling the jugs of water out of the employee bathroom where they'd been stored for the night.

Two guests, Zac and Sonia, arrived home from a morning walk. She was a beautiful woman in a Lauren Bacall sort of way. She even managed to make smoking look sexy.

"We'll help," she offered.

"No, you guys relax and enjoy yourselves," Craig answered, pulling his lips back in what passed as a smile, as he lugged four jugs of water towards the garden to water the plants. Waste not want not.

"Seriously. We'd love to. It'll be fun." Zac persisted.

"Great!" I nearly shouted, excited that my paying guests were offering their help.

"No," Craig said, putting his foot down.

"We insist," Sonia said sweetly. I smiled and figured they just wouldn't take no for an answer - not that I'd actually tried giving it. Craig glowered, but thankfully said nothing more.

The afternoon improved drastically, probably because quite a bit of tasting was necessary. Even Craig managed a chuckle as, through trial and a lot of error, we figured out how to get the cocktails in the garbage can back into the water jugs. It involved a funnel, a bowl and a lot of spillage.

"Here they come!" someone shouted from the street. We all grabbed jugs of liquor and headed for the tables. Jen and Kevin covered the first table, God bless them, and Sonia and I were at the second. Craig sat on the porch and smoked a cigar with Zac. I figured he'd earned the break.

Soon, an amiable crowd of local drunks in all variety of costumes wandered down the block. I heard a familiar voice and glanced up to see a drag queen in his mid-50s with a crooked wig and uneven orange blush tottering towards me on three-inch heels.

"Phil?" I asked.

"Susan!" he exclaimed grabbing my hand between his two beefy ones. "It's so nice to finally meet you!"

Phil owned a guesthouse around the corner from us and we spoke nearly every day on the phone. It was the only time I met him in person and I wouldn't recognize him again if I ran him over with my car.

But I did like his red sequined evening gown. Very snazzy.

    I poured drinks like mad for about twenty minutes, sweating of course, and never again looking up. Beside me, I heard Sonia, the absolute picture of composure, say over and over, "Compliments of Sue and Craig. Next time you have a relative in town, please consider us. Enjoy!"

Visiting Colleagues

Gene and Jeannie were our guests in late March. They were the on-site managers for a guesthouse in Mobile, Alabama. As far as I could tell, they were given pretty much free reign, as the owner was mostly missing. We'd agreed to discount their room – a kind of industry courtesy that, I swear to God, you almost always lived to regret. In Jeannie's case, this came to pass before she'd even arrived. Several times a week I received e-mails from her with helpful breakfast recipes and suggestions that perhaps I'd like to serve one of them while they were in town. When I failed to respond to each and every e-mail, she'd call to follow up. It would seem that in her mind we were a regular Julia Child and Betty Crocker, communicating over the Internet.

Jeannie's husband, Gene, was a severely overweight man. He had round bulging eyes that put me in mind of Craig's favorite TV fishing show that aired on Sunday mornings at 7 a.m. Invariably, the fisherman star of the show caught some unusual breed of deep-water fish that had lived under thousands of pounds of water for many years, had some strange prehistoric spikes all over its body, and had spent its entire life in the pitch black of the deep blue sea. When this fish came to the surface, its eyes literally popped out of its head. Apparently, something to do with the pressure change. No offense intended, but Gene's eyes seemed just shy of popping out. Gene also loved to talk and he loved to drink - as long as he was always drinking somebody else's liquor. Jeannie seemed to have only one thing in common with her husband: she, too, loved to talk. Jeannie was thin, rail thin, and informed us tightly on her first afternoon that she considered drinking a sin. Yes, she used the word, "sin."

My husband, who had been raised in an atheist household, lifted his glass of afternoon red wine to her and smiled benignly. It occurred to me that he didn't actually know what the word "sin" meant.

"In our guesthouse," Jeannie continued, as the web of wrinkles tightened around her pursed lips, "We don't allow guests to drink."

Gene nodded his agreement as he reached out with a meaty fist and grabbed our bottle of wine, refilling his glass generously.

"Hmm..." I answered Jeannie as noncommittally as I could manage. I was the only one at the table who seemed inclined to even acknowledge that she'd spoken.

"Susan," Jeannie addressed me directly, obviously encouraged by the apathetic noise I'd made in her direction and possibly by my fleeting, accidental eye contact.

"Would you like to see the lovely items I've purchased from the art fair today? I'm going to sell them in our gift shop."

Visiting Colleagues

I raised the corners of my mouth in what I hoped would pass for a smile and swallowed a sigh. Of course, I'd want nothing more than to peruse the items the ever-brilliant Jeannie deemed worthy of purchasing at retail prices in arguably one of the most expensive markets in the South to turn around and try to sell in arguably one of the least expensive markets in the South. As she ceremoniously unwrapped the first of her three items, I entertained myself by envisioning the dust collecting on what could only be an extensive collection of her travel souvenirs laid out on the shelves of her guesthouse gift shop. The owner must be so pleased.

Jeannie reached into her Designer Key West Gift Shop Bag that quite possibly cost more than whatever it held and removed a small bundle. She carefully unwrapped a layer of tape and tissue paper, then bubble wrap.

After endless moments of anticipation, she revealed her first purchase: a small wooden plaque, painted Island Pink, with neatly printed black letters. "A woman is like a teabag," it proclaimed. "She gets stronger when she's in hot water!"

"Isn't it charming!" Jeannie proclaimed, handing it to me and watching me expectantly.

"It is!" I agreed, flipping it over and noting the $27.95 price tag on the back. "It's just delightful!" What a steal for a 4x4 inch piece of painted wood.

I waited while Jeannie struggled with the next package. More tissue paper, more bubble wrap, and then a small tin painted gecko was exposed.

"It was made in Africa!" Jeannie announced, inexplicably lowering her voice to a hushed whisper when she said the continent's name.

Craig reached across the table and casually picked up the gecko. He turned it on its back and read the tag on its stomach. "Says here it was made in Taiwan," he announced to nobody in particular.

Jeannie's lips tightened in what was becoming a characteristic expression. A slight flush rose on her pale face. She opted not to answer.

I reached across the picnic table and snagged my pack of Marlboro Lights. Jeannie's smile faded fast. "We don't allow smoking at our guesthouse," she told me, staring pointedly at the lighter in my hand, roughly a half-inch away from the tip of the cigarette in my mouth.

"Hmm," I flicked the bic, so to speak, and inhaled deeply.

"Well," Jeannie stood up and re-packed her bag. "I'm going

upstairs to take a nap." She stared hard at Gene for the first time since she'd arrived at the table. He studied the flowers in the pot straight in front of him as if he might later be quizzed. "Are you coming, Gene?" she finally spat in his direction.

"Oh, for Christ's sake, okay," he replied, slamming his glass of wine (third glass, our treat, if anyone's counting) to the table and shoving his chair back with so much force that Craig had to reach out and grab it to keep it from tipping off the upper deck.

They disappeared inside the house as I turned a conspiratorial smile at my husband. He glared at me in response.

"What?" I asked, feeling a bit offended.

He pointed silently after the retreating Gene and Jeannie.

"What?" I repeated huffily.

"That is why I will never - never - stay in a B&B. So don't you ever bring it up again." Jesus. You'd think I'd been plotting a two-week trip along the Eastern seaboard with a different B&B for every night. He took a healthy swallow off his wine and stomped away from the table to water the plants.

The next afternoon, Craig and I sat down at the back table to share a quick ice water and chat briefly about the morning's events. This was an afternoon habit that was nice as it was usually our only time alone at the house - Maria was gone for the day, our new check-ins had not yet arrived, and current guests were out enjoying paradise.

Jeannie arrived at the table within moments of us sitting down. I couldn't even say for sure where she'd come from. I suspected she'd been waiting for us in the nearby foliage - maybe wearing a hat made from palm-fronds as camouflage.

Today, however, this was not a problem. I smiled at her, listened to her tell a brief and disjointed tale of how Gene had somehow managed to get their car towed and wouldn't be back for hours, and then I sweetly reached in my back pocket for a cigarette. It had exactly the effect I was looking for. She darted away from the table like a mosquito who's spotted a can of Deep Woods Off, shouting over her shoulder something about "nap time."

"Nice one," Craig commented slowly, reaching for his own cigarette.

"Thank you," I responded at once, feeling quite pleased with myself.

No kidding, we couldn't have been sitting there four minutes when Gene came huffing up the side steps, his underarm sweat rings having grown so large it appeared they might compromise and meet in the middle.

"You got a beer?" he managed to get out between big wheezing breaths.

I nodded and jumped up to get him one. While inside, I also snagged a couple of glasses of wine for my husband and myself. I wasn't sitting through a Gene or Jeannie story without a little help. I figured, rightly, that Craig wouldn't mind.

"So," Craig was saying as I came back out. "What happened?" He peered at Gene with his "most-concerned" look.

"Well, seeing as it's Sunday, I figured we could park at the bank. You know. At home, bank opens the lot on Sundays, seeing as they're not using it. Guess that's not true 'round here. Not like I was the only car, though. There were a bunch. So it looked okay to me. Anyways," he paused very briefly to down half his beer in one swallow. "I parked at the goddamn bank and that son-of-a-bitch tow truck came out of nowheres – grabbed me first. Else I would have gotten away. You got another?" He finished off the Budweiser and belched.

I got him another beer.

"Got lucky, though," he continued without so much as a nod of thanks, perhaps he had mistaken me for one of the many waitresses we had running around our backyard, "Copper came along, gave me a ride to the impound."

"Great – that's Key West for you," Craig never missed an opportunity to sing the praises of his beloved adopted town.

"Yeah, would have been great, 'cept this copper was a faggot!" he exclaimed.

Craig and I both winced and shot panicky glances around our small yard and the neighboring property. This was not a word you used in Key West.

"That's right," Gene repeated loudly, just in case the entire Gay Community of Key West had somehow managed not to hear him, "A faggot!"

Craig and I must have looked like someone was throwing pebbles at us, the way we were ducking and cringing.

"I had a feeling," Gene swigged at the new beer. "So when he's talking on his phone, honey this and sweetheart that, then, he hangs up, I says to him, hope that was your girlfriend. Know what he says to me? No such luck, sweetheart! Can you believe the balls on this guy?"

I think, at this point, we could have caught flies with our wide-open mouths. Finally, Craig managed to stutter, "Well, he sounds like a really nice guy."

"Hell yeah. But I hate faggots." No shit. "Gotta say, though, we got to the lot and he told the guy that I was his uncle. Can you believe it? Really helped me out. Saved me two hundred bucks."

He finished the beer and looked longingly at the kitchen.

"Jeannie was looking for you," I lied quickly, taking advantage of his pause and feeling like I needed a hot shower and a new job.

"Ahh shit." Gene shoved off from the table and headed into the house, leaving his empty beers for the mysterious waitress (read: me) to come along and clean up for him.

Craig and I stared at each other. Once again, certainly not the first time, certainly not the last, the guesthouse had left us speechless. The dryer buzzed and we swallowed the last of our wine. It was time to fold the laundry.

Hurricane Charley

There was a hurricane coming. To Key West! We stared dumbstruck at the TV as Bill Kamal, the weatherman on Channel 7, spoke soberly to us about the predicted path of Hurricane Charley. Key West was dead center in the cone of probability. For those unfamiliar with hurricane watching, the cone of probability is a yellow cone overlaid on a map of the Caribbean and the U.S. It shows the meteorologists' best guess of where a hurricane is headed. In other words, it allows you to speculate from the comfort of your living room exactly how screwed you could expect to be in the very near future. And while Bill cautioned us not to focus on the center of the cone, I couldn't help but want to go into the bathroom and throw-up.

We immediately learned about "hurricane sleep" – you go to bed after the last update at 11 p.m. and wake up for the first update at 5 a.m. In the middle, you have nightmares about hurricanes if you're lucky enough to sleep at all. It is a study in sleep deprivation, and, admittedly, makes everybody a bit edgy.

So, it was midnight and we'd discussed the hurricane in great detail, even going so far as to dig out the book I'd bought when we first moved to the island – Hurricanes: Preparation, Survival and the Aftermath. Considering our complete and utter lack of knowledge or experience with hurricanes, eventually we ran out of steam and decided to try and grab a couple hours of sleep before the morning.

The 5 a.m. update was just as bad. The good news, according to the morning weather girl, who quite honestly didn't inspire the same confidence as good old Bill, was that Charley was going to be a Category One hurricane when he reached us. You know, sustained winds of only about 80 mph. Having never been in a hurricane I tried to envision what these winds would feel like. I thought of trying to stand on top of our car as Craig drove down the highway at 80 mph. Sure, no big deal.

The time came to head off to work. Unsure of what we should be doing, Craig and I decided on a divide-and-conquer approach to hurricane preparations. He stayed at our house to move all outdoor objects inside and start the boarding-up process. We'd never had to do this, so it had yet to occur to us exactly how difficult it actually was. In the meantime, as the plan went, I would go to the guesthouse and try to figure out what the hell to do.

My first instinct, when confronted with a new situation, is to run to somebody who knows what they're doing and follow their advice like the gospel. This irritates Craig to no end as he is under the impression we should think for ourselves. Whatever.

Accordingly, when I got to the guesthouse I shouted a quick "Hello!" to Maria and Nina and the few bleary guests wandering about, and sprinted down the street to a neighboring guesthouse.

"Penny!" I cried upon arrival, panting hard. "What are you doing about the hurricane?"

"What hurricane?" she asked calmly, taking in my disheveled appearance, obvious panic, and probably more obvious smell of wine on my breath. Somehow, a morning drink had seemed in order.

She tapped on her computer and pulled up the National Weather Service Web site. "Hmm..." she pondered, studying the cone.

"This is nothing," she finally announced. "Take it easy, I'm not even boarding up for this. Even if it hits us, a Cat 1 is no big deal. A little wind, a little rain. That's all."

A little wind, a little rain. This was something I would hear over and over again from locals who had gone through many hurricanes. Somehow, it never actually managed to comfort me. I was under the distinct impression that the pure definition of a hurricane was something along the lines of wind and rain.

"What do we do?" I asked Penny breathlessly.

"Nothing - don't sweat it. If it's serious we'll get a TA."

Admittedly, I had know idea what a TA was, but I figured correctly that I'd know one when I saw it. I walked calmly back over to my house, determined to relax and greet my guests. It was a beautiful day in paradise - bright blue skies, puffy white clouds, flowers blooming all around. All was well with the world.

With my newfound feeling of smug security, I even called my husband and told him to stop working on our house and come over to the guesthouse. I was feeling ridiculous over our morning panic. There was nothing to fear.

As I passed my office, there was a piece of paper on the fax machine. Over the upcoming month, I would become unfortunately familiar with the format - gray on top with black text that announced "Tourist Advisory." Mystery solved. On the right side of the page there was a small map of the Caribbean that illustrated the cone of probability. The title was followed up with a number and a block of text that informed all hotel owners of the current orders regarding the hurricane.

I had just received TA #1. By the end of Hurricane Charley, we hit forty-three. The last TA we received before the hurricane read something like this: "This will be our last transmission. Good luck to you all." In the middle of the night I stood at the fax machine and cried. Our final link to the outside world had just been severed.

TA #1 announced a non-resident evacuation of the Lower Keys. Okay, it seems self-explanatory, but I managed to stay a little confused. Following instinct, I called Penny on the phone.

"Did you get this?"

"Yeah, it's ridiculous, but we've gotta evacuate the guests. I'm not forcing anyone out till tomorrow, though. This is just plain over-reaction," Penny informed me, still the picture of calm.

"Are you boarding up?"

"No way...not over a Cat 1," she repeated.

Right then Craig showed up. I hung up the phone and passed him Tourist Advisory #1. He read it grimly. "What do we do?"

In a voice that was quick with panic, I informed him of what our neighbors were doing. The hurricane was less than 48 hours away.

"Evacuate the guests," he told me in a dead calm tone that, in my opinion, belayed a deeply seeded layer of fear. Or maybe he really was just being composed in the face of disaster.

"Those guys aren't evacuating their guests till tomorrow," I suggested tentatively.

He gave me a scathing look that belied his feeling on me taking advice from others. "Evacuate the guests," he repeated. "We have two houses to close up and get ready. We can't do anything with people in this house."

He had a really good point; I had to admit. We had shutters to close and plants and lawn furniture to bring inside - at both locations. Of course, little did I know, this didn't actually cover the half of it.

We delivered the bad news to our guests, and although we gave them the option of staying till the next morning if they had to, we strongly encouraged them to pack up and leave as soon as possible. Then we retired to the front porch to plot our next move over a V-8 and cigarette. Almost immediately, two kids in their early twenties carrying backpacks walked up to the house. They were dressed in wrinkled T-shirts and numerous tattoos. Not to mention various body piercings. They looked exhausted.

I think we stared. We didn't mean to, but we'd just finished giving our whole house their marching orders and, quite honestly, nobody had thought to check the possibility of an incoming guest. Which, of course, is exactly what Jack and Alma were.

"Hey," Jack greeted us, walking up the front steps with a lit cigarette in his hand. My first thought was that they must have come off the ferry. It was a four-hour boat ride that ran between Ft. Meyers and Key West. The guests on the ferry generally packed light – explaining only their backpacks.

"Hi," Craig responded unenthusiastically. It was 11:30 a.m. - almost exactly twenty minutes after we'd received the order to evacuate our guests. We were both already exhausted, more from no sleep and the thought of what we had to do than actually having accomplished much.

"You guys know where the office is? We need to check in." Jack looked at us expectantly.

I bounced to my feet, instinct taking over. "Sorry, I can help you. Did you come in on the ferry?" I asked, more to make conversation and cover my momentary confusion.

"Nah...we've been on a bus for the past 33 hours to get here. Came in from Cincinnati." Jack pulled deeply on the butt of his cigarette then flicked it towards the street.

Craig and I exchanged looks of pure distress. These kids had obviously saved all their money and ridden a Greyhound for the past 33 hours only to arrive in Key West and get turned around. You couldn't even fault them, the hurricane had sprung up unexpectedly, leaving residents and tourists alike all but unaware of its presence. They couldn't have known. Unfortunately, it didn't change our circumstances. Nor theirs.

"Oh shit," I sighed, "I'm so sorry, guys. We just got a mandatory evacuation order for all non-residents."

Jack and Alma looked at me blankly, obviously not comprehending how this might apply to them.

"There's a hurricane coming," I offered helpfully.

Their expression didn't change.

Craig came immediately to the rescue, grasping exactly what the situation called for. "You guys want a beer?"

They nodded gratefully and we settled them on the back porch. We started back into an explanation of their circumstances using full sentences and trying to avoid technical terms such as "non-resident evacuation" – something that had confused me less than an hour earlier. In addition, we were aided somewhat, I think, by the fact they had not been checked in nor shown to a room. Even considering their tired state and relative lack of hotel experience, this must have been somewhat suspect and caused them to pay a bit more attention.

Of course, Jack and Alma's lack of funds was truly disturbing. Apparently, when the city ordered an evacuation of the tourists, there was some sort of innate assumption that they all could afford to do so. Such was not the case with the Cincinnati Kids. They had no way off the island and no funds with which to change their vacation plans in mid-stream. We all sat out under the bright blue sky, sipping late-morning/early afternoon cocktails, chain-smoking and calmly debating possible solutions as Hurricane Charley roared towards us from across the Atlantic.

Finally, it was settled. They would stay the night for free so they could afford a rental car to drive up the coast to safety, and then return to finish their vacation after the hurricane had passed. Somehow, Craig and I managed to talk quite arrogantly about post-hurricane conditions as if we had a clue – perhaps it was the cocktails speaking for us.

It was a huge relief to have constructed a plan for Jack and Alma. They ventured into the town blissfully, hand-in-hand, ready to enjoy what remained of a perfectly lovely afternoon. Because all of our other guests had opted to leave that day, and because Nina and Maria had promised to arrive early the next morning for the securing of all outdoor objects, Craig and I decided to focus on the closing of shutters.

Our first discovery (but sadly not our last) was that the hurricane shutters at our guesthouse were screwed open. Understand that most hurricane shutters have hardware that clips them open and therefore closing them is not much of an ordeal. Lean out the window, unclip, close and secure. Such was not the case. Craig had to go up on a thirty-foot ladder with a drill and unscrew the shutters to close them. Okay. Fair enough. What seemed quite unfair was the discovery that the window air-conditioning units in all of our rooms were in the way. They all had to be removed. Sure, even the smallest observation by us prior to this point would have revealed the problem. Whatever.

As we worked our way toward the top floors, we couldn't help but notice the heat increase was much more substantial than usual. Of course, as each unit was removed from below the whole house heated up. Grimly, and naively hoping it would never again be necessary, we noted to ourselves that in the future we should start at the top and work our way down. Adding to the natural oven-like quality of the guesthouse, time of day did nothing to help us. The late afternoon sun blazed through the windows that housed the units, so that eventually our perspiration was no longer even salty – just water running straight out of our pores. It was as if we had both sprung leaks. The final straw turned out to be that many of the A/C units in the house were upwards of twenty years old, meaning they weighed somewhere in the neighborhood of a small Japanese automobile.

So, somewhere around five-ish we'd finally finished the removal of all the A/C units with the exception of the one in Jack and Alma's room. On to the next big surprise! Our shutters had no hardware with which to secure them closed. Yes, it should have been obvious considering the lack of hardware securing them open. But, ask yourself, do you know how hurricane shutters work? We didn't.

Considering the hour and the lack of progress made on our own house, which my husband was determined to blame me for, we decided to head home and get something done there. We figured we'd finish tackling the guesthouse problems after a good night's sleep. And, I can't help but admit that there was a very large part of us that hoped the next update might show all of our work was in vain and no further preparation would be necessary. Fingers crossed!

We awoke on schedule the next morning at 5:10 a.m. after a lovely four and a half hours of rest. We knew the news wouldn't be good as Bill flickered onto the TV in place of the morning weather girl. We were not wrong. There had been some minor changes in the hurricane overnight. Now, Bill informed us in our pre-dawn living room, we could expect winds to pick up by early evening. This was contrary to previous predictions of sometime the following early morning. And, in case that didn't make your stomach clench, Charley was expected to be a Category 2 by landfall in Key West.

It is absolutely amazing what adrenaline can do to a person. Me, Craig, a ladder and a make-shift hammer fashioned from the handle of a chum-grinder managed to fasten all of the boards over our windows before 8 a.m. Our only problem, and some would say not so minor, was that we were about six boards short of actually closing up our house. With no time to stand in line at the local hardware store for more plywood, we reacted quite logically. We got out a compass and determined from which direction the hurricane was coming. The windows on the opposite side of the house were left unboarded. Somehow, the concept of circular winds, the kind an average kindergartner could probably determine by watching the swirling motion on the TV, had escaped us completely. Proud of our work, we indulged in a quick glass of wine and headed for the guesthouse.

As we rode into work on our scooter, I couldn't help but notice the B&B down the street from us (the "we're not boarding up for this!" people) was completely boarded up with a hand-printed sign on the door that said "Closed due to Hurricane Charley." My feelings of dread deepened. Luckily, Nina and Maria had beat us in by about an hour, and a fair amount of the outdoor stuff had been brought inside and crammed into every possible space. It never looked like that much when it was spread out over the backyard, but inside it left us little room to even pass each other in the hallway.

Craig had developed a wonderful plan for the securing of our shutters. We set about it immediately. It involved pulling the shutters shut from the inside and then tying them to each other with fishing wire.

"Hey," he reasoned, "It'll hold a fifty pound fish." Sure, I thought, why not?

Although, I have to admit that at one point when the wire broke as I attempted to complete the knot, I did start having some doubts as to its ability to hold up in the winds. I set this thought aside. We didn't have the time nor the resources to change plans. I told myself firmly that there must have been a faulty spot in the wire and carried on.

Maria took off around noon, declaring the house was pretty much ready to go. I looked around and couldn't help but notice that there were still a fairly large number of items sitting about the backyard. I mentioned this to Craig.

"Don't worry about this stuff," he commented lightly, "I don't care if it gets broken."

"They're potential missiles!" I screamed at him, the very picture of pre-hurricane panic and exactly what our Hurricane Preparedness book warned against – I could have been the poster child.

"Yeah, maybe, " he conceded doubtfully.

"Yes! Yes! They will go flying!" I was flailing my arms wildly to accentuate my point. Very helpful, I'm sure.

"Okay," he exclaimed, exasperated. "Have Nina move this stuff in while we get back to our house and get the dogs and all the supplies." I gave Nina directions, consciously keeping my arms tight to my sides. I smiled ferociously at her, attempting to convey a calm worry-free attitude. She recoiled slightly and averted her eyes.

Leaving Nina to the task of gathering the remaining items of junk from the yard, Craig and I headed home for a quick lunch and final securing of our personal junk in our own yard. Our living room was dark and filled wall to wall with things like leftover shingles, pin-fish traps, pool supplies, gardening tools, outdoor furniture, the cooler that had broken off the back of the scooter, the basket that had broken off the back of the scooter, and other such miscellaneous items. At a time like this, you really had to wonder why you had kept any of it. There is nothing like a hurricane to inspire a commitment to the paring down of outdoor items.

We piled our suitcases, some canned goods and our meager water supply, which I was quite convinced was terribly inadequate, into the back of the car. As there was no room for the dogs, I walked them down to the guesthouse while Craig drove the truck.

Nina's boyfriend, Bud, had come over in our absence to help Nina with our final preparations. I admit I got a little teary when we arrived to find nearly all of the work finished. We all settled down into the room where Craig and I planned to ride out the storm and drank a couple of beers. We were as ready as we were going to get, and in our vast ignorance, we figured we were pretty good.

Soon, Bud and Nina left, toting a roll of borrowed duct tape to finish their own minor preparations. As renters, their landlord had already done pretty much everything.

Craig and I were left alone. The one thing you don't anticipate about a hurricane is how deadly boring it is prior to the storm. Old Bill had been wrong, the winds were not picking up. And although we were lucky enough to have power, at this point the only thing on any of the TV stations was the hurricane. Not that you could concentrate on anything else anyway. So you sit, hour after hour, behind boards, watching the weather on TV. We had lived in terror pretty constantly for the past two days, and now there was nothing to do but sit and wait. Every now and again we'd walk outside, but all there was to see were other buildings, spooky under the glowing streetlights and misty rain, boarded up and looking deserted. Of course they weren't. There were people behind pretty much all of those pieces of plywood. But rarely did you see one.

Finally, around 2 a.m. we dozed off. The hurricane had slowed down again and looked as if it would hit sometime in the morning. I woke up at five, on the dot, and slipped over to the TV. I killed the volume and turned it on, hoping not to wake my husband who, quite honestly, could have used some sleep. The bright neon glow of the TV filled the room, and I stood about three inches away as I couldn't find my glasses and that's about how good my eyesight is.

Hurricane Charley was right below us on the screen – an enormous swirl of bright reds, yellows and purples moving north. And a little west! Yes! A little west!

"How's it look?" my husband's voice came from behind me, soft and low as if afraid of waking the non-existent guests.

"Better," I answered cautiously, moving to the side so that he could see the screen. I went into the bathroom and put my contacts in. It

Diary of a Key West Innkeeper

was obvious we were up for the duration.

Outside, we could hear the rain and wind whistling as the outer bands of the hurricane approached us. We went out and stood on the porch for a bit. The wind was strong, and came from all directions. We made a mental note for future hurricanes – boarding one side of a house is not sufficient.

But it wasn't terrible. It was just the edge as the eye passed 70 miles to our west. We lost power for a brief time while Charley slipped past us. And then we spent the rest of the morning waiting for the remaining outer bands to pass. Sirens went off every couple of minutes. Around noon, we stood on the porch again, as our neighbors straggled by in yellow slickers, heading for the bars at the docks.

"Time for a drink," they commented over and over.

We agreed, and headed back inside for a bottle of wine. We toasted our good fortune and were slightly giddy between the euphoria, wine and lack of sleep. My cell phone rang, which it had been doing nonstop since before dawn, and I answered it expecting another friend or relative from outside the tropics to be calling to check on us. It wasn't. It was our good friend Stella who managed the guesthouse down the street and had weathered the storm in her own home a couple of blocks away. She invited us over for drinks and cards. We told her we would try to make it, but we also wanted to get a head start on putting the house back together. Not to mention, we were expecting Jack and Alma back sometime that afternoon. Before she hung up, she had one last thing to tell us.

"You know," she said in a dead-tired voice. "There's another one coming off the coast of Africa."

And so it began again. Key West was in the cone of probability for four major hurricanes in August and September – Charley, Frances, Ivan and Jeanne. It was as if Mother Nature was a little buzzed and using us for target practice – cause amazingly, she kept missing. Two of them, Charley and Ivan, were expected to landfall in Key West. Ivan was a Category 5 Hurricane. A Cat 5 Hurricane is defined as total destruction. For the other two, Frances and Jeanne, we fell out of the cone of probability at the last minute and turned into the safe zone – hosting two housefuls of evacuees.

We spent nearly two months afraid, and then guilty, as we watched the destruction on TV that had been destined for us. Now it is October, and the ocean seems quiet. Here's hoping it stays that way. Have a drink, send a donation and pray that target practice is over and all of Florida can take the boards down and breath a sigh of relief. Until next year.

Black Flies

We were coming back to work after a day off. A real day off. A true, no-phone-calls, no-emergencies, no-last-minute-crises kind of day off. We had not seen nor heard from our staff in 24 glorious hours. We thanked God for our two-member team that had obviously handled everything in our absence.

We entered the house jovially.

I turned on the computer and, while waiting for it to boot, read the notes that Nina had left for me.

> *Good Morning!*
> *Please water the front garden, I didn't have time.*
> *The guests in Hibiscus need to pay for a bike rental.*
> *Please tell Bamboo they are confirmed for dinner tonight at Cafe Sole - 7pm.*
> *Check Gracie's for FLIES.*
> *Have a great day!*
> *P.S. All the guests are really sweet!!!*

The computer beeped at me, letting me know it was awake. I felt like maybe I wasn't. I reread the note, several times. I stared at one line for a long time. "Check Gracie's for FLIES." I pondered it. What was that supposed to mean?

I went to find Maria. She was cooking. She smiled widely at me.

"Good morning Soo-san," she greeted me. "Do you have a nice day off?"

"Buenos Dias, Senorita. We did, thank you. How was your day?"

"It was a beautiful day!" she informed me enthusiastically.

"Do you know anything about flies in Gracie's Green Room?" I asked her, after what felt like an appropriate pause.

"Si. Big black flies!" she answered, putting emphasis on big. She held her thumb and forefinger in front of my face, spreading them about an inch apart. Indicating the size of the flies?

"A lot of them?"

"Mucho," she said matter-of-factly, flipping a pancake. "But we kill," she added.

I tried to take this in. "Is anyone staying in the room?"

"No. Check-in today. We go see room after breakfast, see if new flies are here."

"I'll go check it now," I countered, still feeling muddled.

She nodded and started garnishing a plate. I left her and walked slowly towards the back cottage. With a feeling of dread, I keyed into the door of Gracie's Green Room.

It was like walking into a scene from the Exorcist.

They were everywhere. Buzzing, crawling, flying. I ducked as they swooped towards my head and ran from the room. They weren't actually an inch long, but they were damn close. And although my Spanish was still extremely limited, I quickly decided that 'mucho' must translate into 'hundreds.'

I rushed back to the kitchen. "Where did they come from?" I asked Maria breathlessly.

She shrugged. "I no know."

"Where did what come from?" Craig asked, having appeared in the side door to the kitchen.

"You have to come out to Gracie's," I told him, pointing in that direction as if he might not remember where the room was located.

He followed me down the back path.

I opened the door and stood to the side. He stepped in.

"Holy shit," he whispered reverently, backing out of the room. He softly closed the door.

We stood and stared, working hard to assimilate what that door contained. Maria came up behind us.

"They back?" she guessed, reading our posture.

"Yeah..." I answered slowly.

"They nasty!" she exclaimed, sticking out her tongue and wrinkling her nose to emphasize her point.

"Yeah..." we agreed somberly.

"Someone's checking in?" Craig finally asked, obviously hoping for the opposite. I nodded my head mutely.

"What time?"

"Late afternoon. They're flying in from Boston." We usually had arrival information on our incoming guests. It helped plan housekeeping. And it came in handy in other situations, such as a Big-Black-Fly-Infestation.

"We're cursed," Craig finally acknowledged sadly.

I nodded again. Even Maria nodded. It was hard to deny the obvious.

"What do we do?" I asked nobody in particular.

"We kill," Maria answered, ever practical.

"But you and Nina killed them yesterday. And they're back."

"Si. But we kill again."

She strode back to the kitchen and returned with a stack of newspapers and a can of Raid. It was for Ants and Flying Insects. I wasn't sure if our flies qualified under that description, but no other ideas were forthcoming. Armed with paper to swat them and poison to kill them, the three of us entered the room. I was starting to believe we may need a priest.

Sometime later, Maria emerged to go find the vacuum. Fly carcasses were everywhere. It was nearly noon. We figured we had between two and four hours until the new guests arrived. And, seeing as how the flies had apparently regenerated after their slaughter the day before, we didn't hold out much hope on the room being ready. Even if it looked good that afternoon, we cringed to think of what surprise might await them upon waking the next morning.

"Do we have another open room?" Craig asked, staring at the small black dead bodies, some of them still writhing.
"Yeah, we've got Starlight. But you know it's not comparable," I told him. It was, in fact, a serious downgrade.

"Okay," he answered slowly, patiently. "But it's not infested with Big Black Flies, correct?"

"True."

"Move them."

"I've only got it open for one night."

"Jesus, Sue. It beats this. Give them a discount. Whatever. Just do it."

I studied the floor, listened to the dying buzz of the flies. He had a point.

I went back to the office and made the adjustments to their reservation, including a hefty "inconvenience" discount. I hoped they were understanding people.

Periodically, I went back to Gracie's to check for signs of life. I know Craig and Nina were doing the same. Around 2 p.m. our vigil was rewarded. The first fly reappeared. The three of us gathered at the back table and talked in hushed, desperate tones.

"There has to be something dead somewhere," I insisted in a whisper. I had grown up in the country. Flies appeared around dead animals. This was a simple fact of life.

As nobody had a better idea, this speculation soon turned to fact. Craig strapped on knee-pads and headed under the cottage to retrieve whatever animal had crawled under the room to die. Thankfully, all of our cats were currently accounted for.

While Craig scooted on his belly in search of a decaying animal, I stood at the perimeter of the cottage and shined a flashlight on him, offering helpful advice. He scowled out at me from the dark, knocked a scorpion off his shoulder, and moved methodically through the dirt. After an extensive search that probably would have made the Army proud, he emerged. There simply was not a dead anything under the cottage.

"What do I tell the new guests about their room change?" I asked him, as he tried unsuccessfully to brush the dirt from his shirt and shorts.

"Make something up," he suggested shortly.

"Obviously. But what?" Prior to owning the guesthouse, lying had never been my strong suit. It was a skill I was quickly acquiring through necessity, but I still occasionally needed help.

"Tell them it's fruit flies. The last guests brought in fruit and we have a fruit fly problem. That doesn't sound so bad."

I agreed. Later we found out, amazingly, this story was not actually far from accurate. The previous guests had brought in fruit. It was the basis in truth that spawned the lie. But, according to a friend at another guesthouse, imported fruit could result in a Big Black Fly Infestation. Who knew?

When I asked the friend's advice, she suggested bombing the room. Not literally. She meant setting off a bug bomb and poisoning everything within its reach. This seemed a brilliant idea until I remembered that Gracie's Green Room shared a lock-out door with Bamboo Hideaway. A door that had a large crack at the bottom. And the Bamboo guests had a dog with them that left the room only rarely for bathroom breaks. I know what you're thinking - put a towel under the door and go to town. But, if you are even remotely familiar with Key West construction you'll have to admit that the cracks in the wooden walls, significant enough to allow hurricane winds to pass through without blowing down, would give you pause. Killing a dog was just not on our agenda.

I asked her if she knew of any alternatives.

Her best idea was to keep killing them, one-by-one. Eventually they would go away.

"How long till they go away?" I asked her.

"Three of four days. Tops." She answered.

Great. Our Boston guests were with us for six days. The first four of which they could expect to be juggled through our open rooms. A new room every night. I tallied the discounts that would be necessary in my head along with the housekeeping costs of stripping a new room daily. I figured it might have been cheaper if they'd never come.

The next morning, after moving the Boston people into another new room (which they were taking surprisingly well), Maria, Craig and I went about the business of killing the flies. We were cautiously encouraged. Their numbers seemed to be decreasing.

After her shift, I found Maria in the kitchen. She was brewing something on the stove. It didn't smell like tomorrow's breakfast.

"What are you making?" I asked, passing through and grabbing a banana for lunch.

"Is good luck," she told me.

"Really?" At odds with everything I'd ever believed in, and in this case, that in which I did not believe, I felt my spirits rise.

"Yes. I spray house around house- Tss! Tss!" She made a noise like a squirt bottle and mimed spraying with her hand.

"Yeah?"

"Bad luck, he go away." She informed me gravely, stirring the mixture.

"Great!"

Finally, a solution.

That night, as Craig and I got drunk on the couch, I informed him happily that our troubles were over.

"Maria has made a special potion for good luck," I told him carefully, trying not to slur.

He flipped through the TV channels and chose not to acknowledge my statement.

"Seriously," I insisted. "She sprayed the outside of the house. It will ward off the evil." I spoke with the authority of too much wine.

Eventually he looked away from the TV and studied me for a moment. He was probably trying to determine either my level of sanity or the level of my buzz.

"Great, Sue. That's just great." He finally said. He continued to flip through the channels. I nodded contentedly, secure that the worst was now over.

Jose Gato Diablo Snuggles

meow

It was a Sunday in December, about a week before our second Christmas, and it was our day off. We woke up leisurely. Made coffee. Went to the bathroom. Where there was no toilet paper. Shit. We were also out of paper towels, which everybody knows will work in a pinch. I was debating the utility of coffee filters when we decided to do what all good guesthouse owners would do. Craig took off on the scooter, headed for Orchids, to procure a couple of rolls. I waited very anxiously for his return.

But he didn't come back. Instead, the phone rang. It was just after 8 a.m. and caller ID let me know the call was coming from Orchids.

"Hello?" I answered cautiously.

An unbelievable yowling filled my ears.

"Sue?" Craig yelled over it.

"What's happening?" I shouted back.

"It's Fred! I think he broke his leg! We have him locked in the bathroom!"

Fred was not our cat. But he did live at Orchids. He had come with the property. Only in Key West do pets pass with a sale. Although unusually, Fred actually did have an owner. Her name was Greta. I think she was German. She had, at one point, lived in the house next door to Orchids. When she sold and moved about a mile away, Fred had refused to leave the guesthouse. So he stayed with us but was owned by her. He was a fiercely independent cat, who started mean and seemed to grow meaner as time passed. He had a torn ear, a scarred face and a fairly constant flea problem. He scratched our guests, fought with the other cats, and declined any affection from anyone but Nina, to whom he'd taken a liking.

"Oh no!" I hollered into the phone. "I'll be right there!"

"No! Call Greta!"

We hung up the phone and I dug out the phone number. She wasn't home, so I left an urgent message with every number I could think of short of 9-1-1. I called back over to Orchids.

"I can't find her!" I shouted over the continued screaming sound of Fred in pain.

"Get a vet!" Craig yelled.

We hung up again.

I rummaged around and found the phone book. Then it occurred to me that I had no idea who Greta used for a vet. Whenever Fred needed anything, we called her and she showed up with a cat carrier and whisked him away. And it was Sunday. No Key West vets worked on

Sunday so there was no way to call around and figure out who had records of Fred.

Hmm...

Desperate, I called the emergency service for the vet we used for our dogs. I explained the crises to the operator who answered.

"Is the cat a current client?" she asked.

"A what?" I answered.

"Is this his first visit or has he been seen here before? The veterinarians will only treat current clients on Sundays," she informed me.

"Yes," I lied easily. "He's a current client." What the hell, I figured, he might be.

Arrangements were made for the doctor to meet us at the office in half an hour. I drove our truck to the guesthouse. I could hear Fred from the street.

Inside, distressed guests milled about. Nobody wanted to eat breakfast, nobody had an appetite with the tortured cries of Fred echoing around the property.

We sent Nina back to her apartment to get a cat carrier. Luckily, she owned two cats of her own and therefore owned a carrier. She bravely loaded Fred inside. As the only person he had any affection for, it seemed the right choice. Plus, let's be honest, I was scared of him.

Craig and I took off for the vet. Fred yowled pitifully from the cage. I started sneezing and wheezing. I was very allergic to cats and the closed car was a near death-sentence for me.

"So much for a day off, " Craig grumbled.

I blew my nose and rubbed my itchy eyes. "Yeah, well."

Our vet answered the door when we knocked. We knew her well, as she had literally saved our dog's life about six months earlier.

"I don't remember ever treating your cat," she commented in mild reproach, raising her eyebrows at me.

I sniffed and confessed. Fred had inconveniently quieted in the carrier. I briefly considered poking him, so she could hear his distress. We needed some sympathy. We needed a break.

"Well," she finally said, "He's here now, let's see what we've got."

We gratefully followed her through the darkened offices into an examining room. It was eerily quiet.

She flipped on the florescent lights in the room. They flickered and came to life. Craig reached into the carrier and pulled out Fred's passive body. He meowed once and fell silent. His right front leg dangled uselessly.

Our vet started an examination. She stopped almost immediately. "Did you give him anything?" she asked. I looked at Craig.

"Just some Baby Tylenol - for his pain," he answered.

She sighed deeply, tiredly, and started asking questions about dosage, milligrams, etc. As her questions became more detailed, I had to get on the phone to Maria so that she could read the bottle's label to us.

Apparently, Tylenol is poisonous to cats. Who knew?

So, poor Fred not only had what we assumed was a broken leg, he had been poisoned as well. By accident. By us.

I held Fred while our vet pumped syringe after syringe of charcoal down his throat.

"What about his leg?" I asked at one point.

"I'm much more concerned about the poison right now," she answered grimly.

I didn't ask any other questions.

Craig wandered away during this ordeal, returning periodically to check on us. An hour or so later, when we were leaving, and leaving Fred behind for further observation and treatment, Craig stopped me at a stack of cat cages in the hallway. The sign over top of them read, "Looking for a Good Home!" A huge beautiful grey cat saw him coming and started purring and rubbing against the bars of his cage. So this was where he'd been spending his time. Craig scratched him the best he could. The cat purred like a car getting going.

I reached a finger through the bars and petted his head. I read the sign on the side of the cage. His name was Snuggles. We stood there for a while before leaving. I think the same thought was in both our heads. "This is the kind of cat a guesthouse should have!" But we wouldn't say it out loud. Not with Fred, poisoned and crippled, sitting just on the other side of the swinging door.

Greta returned our phone call late that afternoon and the financial and emotional care of Fred was happily turned over to her. Throughout the next couple of days, we got updates. He did not have a broken leg. He had a tumor, under his front leg. It had cut off all feeling to the leg, therefore giving it the appearance of being broken. He'd recovered nicely from the poisoning. But there was a problem. Greta could not take him home. She had another cat - Fred's brother or cousin or father or something - who was very old and very diabetic. She didn't think she could handle Fred.

Jose Gato Diablo Snuggles

First instinct: This is our problem because...?

Second instinct: Poor Fred. What are we going to do?

We couldn't take Fred back without a functioning front leg. A cat at a guesthouse must be able to defend himself. Fred just couldn't.

The phone rang.

It was Tammy, the previous owner's wife.

"I was at the vet today with one of our cats," she told me after we exchanged greetings.

"Yeah?"

"Was that Fred in there?" Apparently, we had the same vet. I told her it was and conveyed the whole story, including Fred's unfortunate new status as homeless.

"I could take him," she started.

"Oh my God! Tammy, that's wonderful!" I shouted into the phone. Yipee! I blessed Tammy's endless reserve of compassion for animals. Problem solved.

"There's just one problem," she continued.

"Oh." I deflated.

"I had agreed to adopt another cat. One at the vet's office. I can't take them both."

I thought about it. Could we be this lucky? "Which cat?" I asked, holding my breath.

"He's a big grey. His name is Snuggles."

Yipee! Again!

"I've got an idea," I said, trying to keep my voice steady, "How about we take Snuggles, and you take Fred?"

We struck a deal. And the sweet cat, the big beautiful grey cat, the perfect guesthouse cat, would soon be ours. We broke the good news to Maria and Nina. An air of happy anticipation electrified the lunch table that afternoon.

We questioned how we would get him to the guesthouse the next day. Nina volunteered. It was her day off. But the wild excitement of a new pet had captured us all.

We started debating his name.

"I don't like Snuggles," I declared.

"I like Snuggles. It's so sweet," Nina argued.

"I think we should name him Jose," I suggested. Maria smiled broadly. For some odd reason, I'd always wanted a pet named either Jose or Sven. I have no idea why.

"Jose Gato," Maria stated. Translation: Joe Cat. It seemed

perfect. But Nina was not satisfied.

"Jose Gato Snuggles," she finally conceded. We all agreed.

That night, each in our own ways, we prepared for the arrival of Jose Gato Snuggles. Basically, we all went to a store. For Jose's first day at Orchids, he would have shrimp treats in the shape of goldfish, balls with bells inside, little cloth animals stuffed with catnip and albacore tuna for lunch.

The next morning, Maria, Craig and I waited in breathless anticipation for Nina to return with our new pet.

When she arrived and opened the cage, Jose Gato Snuggles darted immediately under the kitchen table. Where he stayed. For hours. We peppered the floor with the shrimp-goldfish and rolled the balls-with-bells at him. He eyed us suspiciously.

Maria, her shift having finished hours earlier, finally gave up and went home. She was a little disappointed. Nina, Craig and I continued the vigil. At one point, we decided perhaps he needed a little time to adjust. We went outside and drank wine at the back table and tried to pretend we weren't watching him. Which we were.

Finally, he ventured out. Slowly, hunkered, eyes turning in every direction. We smiled quietly at each other and continued talking as if he might notice if we stopped.

After several moments, Craig went softly inside. Jose flinched, but held his ground.

Craig laid down on the kitchen floor in a non-threatening sort of way. More time passed. Then Jose approached him. Slowly. And he started purring. Craig ran his hand up and down Jose's body as the cat rubbed against him. He smiled out the back door at us, gave us a thumbs up.

With no warning, Jose suddenly spun and sank his teeth into Craig's hand. Deep. Into the meaty part near the thumb. Craig screamed in pain and Jose darted out the open back door.

Jose Gato Snuggles disappeared. I cannot say we went looking for him.

The next morning, when we told Maria what happened, she said, "Diablo! Diablo! You know?"

"Devil?" I guessed.

"Si. Jose Gato Diablo," she concurred.

Craig's hand swelled and turned an angry red. He could not make a fist nor grip anything. He was taking loads of aspirin to kill the pain. The day before Christmas Eve I managed to talk him into going to the clinic. I was afraid that if we waited they would be closed and we'd end up spending Christmas Day in the Emergency Room.

The doctor at the clinic agreed when he saw my husband's hand. He put him on a massive dose of antibiotics, wished him luck, and told him to beware of a red line running up his arm and heading for his heart. Great.

Christmas morning arrived and Craig and I went to Orchids to prepare breakfast. This year, Maria had her family back in town and had taken the day off.

Jose Gato Diablo Snuggles was waiting at the front door. I couldn't figure out for sure how he had found his way back, but I suspected that the shrimp-flavored-goldfish had made an impression. We let him in. I gave him a can of tuna fish and didn't try to pet him. Craig scowled at him from a distance.

Jose never bit anybody again. This is not to say that all of us didn't hold our breath when a guest scooped him up to cuddle, or when we found out that someone had taken him into their room and slept with him in their bed, a frequent occurrence that we whole-heartedly discouraged. We loved him dearly while living in fear of his next unprovoked attack.

Diary of a Key West Innkeeper

A Penny Saved

It was a Thursday. I know this because Thursday was the day that Maria came in to start breakfast and housekeeping, and then had to leave by 9:30am to make it to her morning classes. We arrived just before nine. Craig went outside to sweep the sidewalks and I went in the house. As I walked down the hallway, instead of hearing Maria's laughter, or her cheerful voice describing the beautiful breakfast she was going to prepare, I heard her sternly questioning a guest. I went immediately to the kitchen.

Maria was standing, hands on hips, frowning severely at the lovely elderly couple that were staying in Hibiscus Room.

"You drink my orange sauce?" she asked them.

They cringed and took an unsteady step back. "No, of course not," the old woman insisted.

"If you do, I find out," she warned them.

"Honestly, we have no idea what you're talking about," the old man answered.

Maria narrowed her eyes and stared hard at them. Silent. After several moments, during which the old couple shifted uncomfortably, she finally relented.

"Okay," she said briskly. "You go sit. I bring you breakfast."

They turned out of the kitchen and doddered as quickly as they could into the gardens.

"Hola Seniorita," I greeted Maria. "What's going on?"

She slammed a frying pan onto the top of the stove and threw a tablespoon of butter at it. Then she turned to me.

"Soo-San!" she exclaimed. "I get here and my batter, she's gone. I no know!" She threw her hands up in frustration and stomped over to the sink.

The batter to which she referred was our L'Orange sauce, used for french toast. You put a couple of raw eggs in a blender along with some orange juice concentrate, a little rum and some milk. It was prepped the day before and sat overnight in the fridge. Apparently, upon arriving that morning Maria had discovered the batter missing. She'd had to dig out an extension cord and take the blender to the sidewalk to remake the batter - she didn't want to disturb sleeping guests by running the blender inside.

"I go do make-up. See if they is lying." She started past me.

"Are lying." I corrected automatically. Maria was intent on improving her English.

She stopped. Cocked her head at me. "Are lying?"

"Yes. They are lying."

"They are lying," she pronounced loudly and clearly.

The elderly couple, seated just beyond the open kitchen door, heard us. The old man blinked rapidly and took his eighty-six year old wife's hand. He whispered something to her and pointed to the fence at the edge of the property. I assumed it was probably an escape plan should events continue to deteriorate.

I smiled reassuringly at them and shook my head dismissively. They didn't seem overly comforted. They'd probably figured out who really ran the house. It wasn't me.

Maria headed down the hallway while the couple's omelets and french toast cooked. She did a speedy make-up on their room. It was something of a small miracle that she could cook somebody's breakfast and do their make-up simultaneously. She was that good.

She came back into the kitchen just when I was sure she was getting ready to burn the eggs. She flipped their meal deftly onto a plate, sculpted a rose out of a strawberry, added a little whipped cream and took off for their table.

"It was no them," she informed me on her way by.

"Okay..." I'd really not thought it had been. They just didn't seem the type.

"I find out."

I nodded. I knew I couldn't stop her, so there seemed no point in trying. Over the next twenty minutes or so, the interrogations continued as each guest came down to breakfast. Then, unsatisfied with their answers, Maria would take off running for their room as soon as they got seated in the garden. I shuddered to think what would happen when she found her culprit. It didn't take long.

"Ah Hah!" She yelled from the third floor. Her footsteps shook the house as she raced down the stairs with the empty L'Orange sauce container clutched in her hand. She ran straight through the kitchen and into the garden.

The young couple that was staying in Starlight Secret looked up in terror.

"Why you drink my batter?" she demanded, planting herself next to their table.

"I didn't know..." he answered lamely.

"I ask you, 'You drink my batter?' and you are lying. You say, 'No, no, I no do.'"

She scowled at them.

"I thought it was orange juice," the young guy finally admitted, hanging his head.

"You were drunkee!" she concluded triumphantly.

He nodded shamefully, not looking up.

"It made him throw-up," his girlfriend offered helpfully.

"Yeah?" Maria asked, tilting her head to one side. Was she to be appeased?

He raised his eyes hopefully. "Yeah, it made me really sick."

Maria laughed heartily, good-humor restored. She patted him firmly on the back. "I get you real orange juice and a beautiful breakfast. You feel better now." She walked off jauntily, singing under her breath. Apparently, this revelation satisfied her sense of justice. All was well. The old couple breathed a sigh of relief.

"I cook for them, poor guy," she told me once back in the kitchen. "Then I go."

"Thank you, amiga." There was nothing else to say. She glowed at me.

She left shortly thereafter, blowing us a kiss and still chuckling. There were only two make-ups remaining. Craig would do them while I finished cleaning up the kitchen.

He started up the stairs to Bahama Blue. Not ten minutes later he was running for the employee bathroom, where I heard him retching. He didn't come out for a long time. Worriedly, I stood outside the door and peppered questions at it. He didn't answer, but I could hear water splashing. At least he was alive.

Finally, the door opened. Craig stepped out, pale. He pushed past me and walked to the outdoor garbage cans. He returned barefoot. It was only about 10am, but he popped open a bottle of wine and downed a glass.

"What happened?" I asked for about the twentieth time.

He refilled his glass. Took a deep breath.

"I was doing the make-up in Bahama Blue," he started. I nodded impatiently. I already knew this.

"I was getting their garbage," he continued after a big swig of his wine.

I nodded again. Was this story going anywhere?

"You know how you sometimes just pick the garbage out, to save the bag?"

Okay, I know it sounds gross to those of you who don't spend your lives cleaning up other people's lives. But it is a reality. After months of housekeeping, you become numb to the things that would have disgusted you in a previous life. And the bags to which he referred, the liners in the little garbage cans in the rooms, weren't free. So, when whatever was inside looked benign, we all did it. Reached in, removed the facial tissue or coke can, and saved the bag.

"Yeah...?" I was starting to get a bad feeling about where this was headed.

"It looked like just a tissue," he shook his head miserably. He stared at his hand. My eyes followed his. I, too, stared at his hand.

"But it wasn't?" I finally prompted.

"No. No. It wasn't." He polished off the second glass of wine and poured a third.

"What was it?"

"It was..." he gulped hard. "It was a condom, full of jizz. It ran down my arm. It dripped on my shoes." He shuddered.

"So your shoes are?"

"In the garbage can!" With these words he was off. Back into the employee bathroom, scrubbing his hand, his arm and, if I had to guess, probably his foot. I reached across the table and downed the remainder of his third glass of wine. Then I giggled. I couldn't help it. He returned to the table. I plastered on a straight face. But he could see the corners of my mouth twitching.

"It's not funny!" he shouted.

I shook my head. "No, it's not," I agreed seriously.

"I hate this job," he growled.

"I'll do the Bamboo Hideaway make-up," I offered. "Just take it easy for a bit."

He nodded glumly and poured another glass.

I walked back to the cottage and knocked on the door of Bamboo Hideaway.

"Housekeeping!" I shouted. When there was no answer, I keyed into their room.

I counted off the five steps of a make-up, just as I was taught. Needless to say, I didn't reach into a garbage can. I had finished everything and was gathering the used towels. On the shelf behind the toilet a dry washcloth was unfolded. I grabbed it with the other towels. A round disk fell out. It rolled around the rim of the toilet that I had not yet flushed and was full of urine. I held my breath. Luckily, it tipped to the outside.

I reached down to pick it up. It was beige, made of hard rubber, and about two inches in diameter. I turned it over in my hand. I wondered if it was a plumbing part that had broken off, or perhaps one of those floor protectors you put under the foot of a bed.

Okay, here we go again. It sounds utterly disgusting, but it is another habit you get into when you do a lot of housekeeping. You have to use all of your senses, with the exception of taste, when trying to determine what something is. So, when stumped, we sniff things. I think this is a habit born from laundry. An unidentified brown stain on a pillow case could be chocolate or mascara. To treat the stain correctly you must ascertain what it is. So you sniff it.

So yes, I brought the little round rubber disk to my face. And I sniffed it. The odor was almost non-existent. But it was there. It took me a second to place...then I threw the diaphragm across the room.

My hands were shaking. I gagged.

I ran from the room, slamming the door closed behind me. I ran past my husband, slightly recovered and still at the kitchen table, and without a word went into the employee bathroom. I scrubbed my hands for many, many minutes.

I came out, finally, still shaky. I told him what happened. He giggled.

"It's not funny!" I shouted.

He shook his head, trying for a straight face. "No, it's not."

"I hate this job," I growled.

"I'll go finish the make-up in Bamboo. Just take it easy for a bit."

I nodded and poured myself a big glass of wine.

(Note: That afternoon I calculated the cost of a small garbage can liner. It turned out to be approximately 1 cent. We took a vote. It was unanimous. It was not a penny worth saving.)

Fight Night

Fight Night

We were working a split shift. Maria and Nina were working the morning, and Craig and I were taking over at noon. It was a rare arrangement that had been born of necessity. It was a Sunday, and the Saturday night before we'd had to stay up past 2 a.m. to watch the UFC.

For those of you unfamiliar with the Ultimate Fighting Championship, it is a brutal series of fights that happens once every three months showcasing the best athletes in the world in a mixed martial arts genre. We loved it and couldn't miss it. We often injured each other the next day practicing the moves we'd learned.

Nina graciously gave up part of a day off to let us sleep in.

When we arrived, Nina and Maria were both upstairs in Bahama Blue. We could hear them, and the guests, in the room. We walked up to investigate.

Nina was holding the fifty-five pound TV in her arms while Maria dragged a table out of the way and then dead-lifted the dorm-sized refrigerator into a corner of the room. Nina gratefully dropped the TV on top of the fridge. They were both sweating buckets.

The guests, repeats from the previous owner whom we had yet to meet, stood and watched. They made lots of gracious noises while they hemmed and hawed and made suggestions and pointed. She wore an immaculate light blue linen dress and a stylish straw hat with matching band. He sported pressed khaki shorts and a golf shirt with a Maui Logo that probably cost about what they were paying for the room.

We hated them immediately.

"Sue and Craig," Nina, the flawless hostess, said as she spotted us and wiped the sweat from her eyes, "Meet Judd and Lisa. They're staying with us from North Carolina."

Everybody spoke at once.

"Hello!"

"Nice to meet you."

"Hello!"

"What the hell's going on?"

I'll give you one guess who said what.

Judd turned a salesman's smile onto my husband. I could have told him it wouldn't work.

"We just love what you've done with the place," he said with true Southern insincerity. "We just needed a couple of small adjustments to make it work for us."

"We're done here," Craig stated flatly, ignoring the smile. Nothing like spending the previous evening watching Chuck Liddel and

Tito Ortiz beat up on each other (a couple of bad-ass 205-lb guys) to put you in a no-nonsense state of mind.

Nina and Maria hesitated. We had always led by example and in their experience we rarely said "no" to a guest request. Obviously, they knew there was more to come on the "small adjustments" list.

"Sure, sure," Judd said, still smiling and not catching the hint. "We just need a mirror over the desk and we'll be pretty much good."

"A mirror over the desk?" my husband repeated.

"Yes. I have some work to do, and I like to have a mirror so I can watch myself."

Craig stared blankly at him.

"I know, I know, sounds silly," Judd laughed in a self-deprecating sort of way. "But my work involves cold-calling and it's a proven fact that you are more animated if you can see yourself." He shrugged amiably.

"Hmm." Craig answered. "Let me ask you a question, Jerry."

"Judd."

"Huh?"

"My name is Judd."

"Right. Judd. When you go to the Hilton to stay, do you require the staff to rearrange your room?"

Judd's smile slid from his face and dropped to the floor at his loafer-clad feet.

I laughed loudly, trying to cover the moment.

"We just don't have a mirror for over the desk," I said loudly. I shot a look at Maria.

"No, no," she agreed quickly, picking up the hint. "We no have mirror."

"Sure we do..." Nina ambled into the conversation.

"No. We don't." I stated, staring her down and willing some level of comprehension.

"How 'bout that one in the employee bathroom?" she continued. I blamed myself. Again, we rarely said no to a guest and she had been trained to please. She was trying to help.

"It broke," I lied, as everyone stared at me.

"Let's go," Craig said briskly, including Nina and Maria in the statement.

The four of us assembled in the kitchen. Craig was on fire.

"What was that? Who the hell do they think they are?"

"I think they're sweet," Nina ventured. I cringed.

He turned to her. "Bullshit. Bullshit." He said,

emphasizing his point with a finger inches in front of her face.

"They stay last year. Repeat. Is good, yes?" Maria waded in.

"I don't want repeats like that. They're assholes! You know 'asshole'?" He stared her down. She nodded and repeated the word clearly to indicate her comprehension.

"That is the biggest load of shit I've seen," he continued. "What next? A brighter night light? Go buy them a painting? Maybe the bed's too soft and they need a new mattress?" He walked to the desk and returned a moment later. He tossed a Crate and Barrel catalogue on the kitchen floor. "Someone take this up to them. Let them pick out a whole new room. What the hell?"

Nina and Maria cowered. They glanced at me. Craig could occasionally be prone to fits of temper. Hell, so could I. Point being, when one of us was losing it, they looked to the other to step in. Fair enough.

I walked up to him. "Enough. Leave it alone."

He rounded to face me. "It's bullshit and you know it!" he shouted.

I crouched into a fighter's stance. A glint came into his eye. He sneered at me. Sometimes, nothing relieves tension like a little wrestling. And, after last night, I was feeling cocky.

"Feeling lucky?" he cooed as he dropped into a crouch. We circled each other in the kitchen. Nina and Maria grinned and started cheering. I heard a side bet taking place. For good reason, odds were not in my favor.

I spun and delivered an awkward, off-balance roundhouse kick towards my husband's stomach. He caught it easy. He twisted my foot into a heel-hook. I screamed in pain but collapsed on the floor forcing the release. He was behind me in a second, shooting for a reverse-naked choke. I dropped my chin and defended.

"Excuse me?" It was our sweetheart guest, Myra, who was traveling alone.

We broke apart sweating and panting. I climbed off the floor.

"Hey, Myra!" I exclaimed, giving her a tin-foil-bright smile.

"I don't want to interrupt..." She glanced around the room. Craig was on his feet now as well. Nina and Maria were exchanging money after a quick soft argument about who had won.

"No problem. We were just playing around!" I grinned furiously at her.

"Sure," she answered skeptically.

"Did you need something?"

"Yeah...I just wanted to rent a bike."

"I can take care of that for you!" I replied enthusiastically. She took a step back. I grabbed the bike rental box and had her fill out a disclaimer. Then I led her out to where we kept the bikes. She chose one and I gave her the key, along with my standard speech.

"Now, Myra, you break by stepping back, follow traffic signals, and remember, bike defensively! Half the people on the road are either drunk or lost, so don't count on them doing what they're supposed to do. Okay?"

"Great," she answered, still eyeballing me warily. She adjusted her seat and climbed aboard.

"Have fun!" I called as she rode down our side path towards the street.

She glanced back at me and waved. Right then, a pedestrian stepped across her path. She wasn't going fast yet, but nonetheless had to swerve unexpectedly. She ran straight into a parked car. The bike stopped abruptly and Myra went flying over the hood.

"Ouch!" I muttered, starting towards the street to see if she was okay.

She bounced up before I got there, gave me another wave, picked up the bike, and took off again. I smiled and waved back. Hell, for all I knew, she could have had a broken ankle but determined that she was safer riding away from the crazy people at her guesthouse than she was seeking their help.

I went back into the kitchen. Craig was waiting.

"Ready?" he asked, cracking his neck as I entered.

I hiked my skirt and resumed a fighting position. I thought I heard "double or nothing" from one of our employees. I felt a glow that someone was betting on me. We circled and resumed.

Should We Stay or Should We Go?

We went. On a blue-sky day in June, we signed the paperwork and sold the guesthouse. Our attorney, who moonlighted at the guesthouse his wife managed, sat with us at the closing table.

"How're you guys feeling?" he asked in his down-home southern drawl.

Craig leaned a little further back in his chair. He stared stoically at our attorney through his sunglasses. I think his morning wine buzz was still in effect. I answered for us both.

"Like crying. I can't believe it's over. I feel like falling down on my knees and thanking God for getting us out. I-"

"Enough, Sue." He cut me off, his soft southern accent taking on a harder edge. "Remember, some of us still have to do it tomorrow."

I apologized. In my own moment of ecstasy, I'd forgotten that where we'd escaped, others had not. I was genuinely contrite. But my heart pounded wildly in my chest.

It was over! It was over!

But was it?

No.

But, perhaps not in the way that after reading these stories you would come to expect.

The Thompsons came back to town. They had been our guests twice over the two years and even though they were twenty years older than us, a bond had formed. They came to our home for cocktails and lunch and we sat in the backyard talking and laughing for nearly eight hours. We are still in touch with them, via e-mail, phone calls and occasional visits. Their home is open to us should we ever decide to head back up North.

We spent our first Thanksgiving without the guesthouse in another guesthouse, where the Green party, who had been with us the previous year, was staying. They'd booked our whole guesthouse for the holiday, but we had to move them to another when we sold. Jack carried his famous stuffing on a plane all the way from North Carolina. The turkey cooked at Nina's house, in the dishes borrowed from ours. We all carried it back to their new guesthouse. And although we did not join in the naked Jacuzzi adventures at midnight, we did enjoy a feast with the dearest of friends and the sweetest of people.

Amber calls me when she's in town, which is often. She was our frequent guest for nearly the entire two years we owned Orchids. She flies to visit Key West from Chicago almost every month and has more friends around town than I do. We used to tell her, and still do, that she could save a lot of money by buying a home here and not paying hotel rates. (You know who you are and you know I'm right!) Now, every so often, we sit out back at Finnegan's Wake and catch up on our lives.

Stan lives in Florida and visits with almost the same regularity as Amber. He was friends both with the old owners and with us. He's now friends with the lovely people who take care of him at his new guesthouse. He calls us when he's coming and brings us gifts of beautiful salmon from his Alaskan vacations that he somehow squeezes in between his Key West vacations. Oh, to live the life of Stan.

Stella, the manager of the guesthouse down the street from ours, the ones who **WERE NOT** boarding up for Hurricane Charley, continues to be our closest friend. We all wait in great anticipation for the new Survivor Series so we have a 13-week long excuse to eat dinner together and gossip every Thursday night. Of course, we don't always need an excuse. I'm sitting on her front deck now as I write these words. It's a very good place to be.

Nina is like a daughter to us, and I believe that we love her in just that way. We are often frustrated because we want her to do the things we think she should do, and when she chooses her own road, we are always proud of what she does. As of this time, she is considering leaving Key West and moving back to Europe. It's a hard choice for her because she loves this little town.

Maria went back to school full time. She calls and stops by to keep us posted. Seeing her always brings a smile to my face and makes me hide my wine glass, depending on the hour. Hurricane Wilma in October, 2006 forced her out of her home with the flooding and she is living in a **FEMA** trailer. She lost her school books along with pretty much everything else. But she's optimistic, because she and her family are safe. Despite the hurricane, she is still a student and has started work with a local nonprofit agency that aids hurricane victims. She created a coloring book to help children that was published by **FEMA** in multilple languages. I'm not sure if they can possibly love her as much as we did, but I am sure that her smile, her dedication, and her humor will be a blessing to the people she now works to help.

There are a thousand more stories. Good and bad. The stories I've told are not the worst of what happened at the guesthouse. There are secrets we will carry to our graves. Neither are these stories the best. Above is the smallest sampling of the guests that became friends, the acquaintances that became best friends and the staff that became family. The stories I've told are the middle of the road, just an average day.

So you want to know what it's really like to own a guesthouse? All I can say about our experience is that we wouldn't change a thing.

And we'd never do it again.

About The Author

Born in a small town outside of Cincinnati, Ohio, Susan graduated college from Miami University with a degree in Psychology. She moved to Chicago and landed a high powered position at Enterprise Rent-a-Car as a Management Trainee. She quit after 2 months. Realizing she had to do something with that expensive Psych degree, she became a cocktail waitress at a billiards bar. Where she met her husband, Craig. With his encouragement, she left the bar and embarked on a real estate career. Seven years later, Susan and Craig decided it was time to take a chance on life and to get out of the cold. So they moved to Key West. They both loved the small town feel and, of course, the cocktail hours, backyard BBQ's, fishing and sun. They bought a guesthouse. They sold a guesthouse. They now live in beautiful St. Augustine, Florida, with their two dogs, Sneaker and Pokey. But home is where the heart is, and for Susan and Craig, Key West will always be home.

Diary of a Key West Innkeeper

Thank You

  This year, my husband and I are celebrating our ten-year wedding anniversary. Yahoo! Through some very hard times, some of which you have read about in the previous stories, he has consistently supported and encouraged my writing. He worked on this book nearly as hard as I did, editing, brainstorming and offering invaluable input. For this, and for so many other things, I thank him and love him dearly.
  In addition, I am eternally grateful to the real "Maria and Nina" for being our family, our friends, our voices of sanity and our saviors throughout our experience as Innkeepers.

I am also very thankful to the following:
Fran, my mother, for your love and support and giving us the time to take some time away from the guesthouse;
Liz, for being a sounding board for this book as well as a wonderful friend and a lovely Thursday night dinner guest along with Buddy;
Jody, for freely sharing your advice and experience, without which we may not have survived our first year;
George, for helping out when we needed it, entertaining our guests with fascinating stories and being a gentle reminder of life beyond the guesthouse;
Thank you to the previous owners of Orchids, for showing us the ropes, continuing to answer your phone and our questions way beyond your obligation to do so and for helping at the house during a terrible time of personal crisis.
Frank the Plumber, for bailing us out more times than I can count, regardless of the hour or the holiday;
Sandy, Frank's Wife, for always picking up our phone calls and always being sweet and patient;
Ignacio, Robert and Angel, our electricians, same reason as Frank;
Tom the Bike Man, just because you're a good guy whose attitude was a constant reminder of what is so special about the Southernmost Town;
Vic the Pool Man, for your expertise and creativity on what had to be the most problematic pools in Key West.

  When we had to evacuate to Fort Lauderdale during Hurricane Ivan, we traveled with the employee of another guesthouse, sharing a room with her and her dog. The B&B owner there was shocked that we would be such good friends. He, too, was a fairly new owner, and told us that competition was tough in Fort Lauderdale. Apparently, the Innkeepers there did not cooperate with each other, no less make friends. I can't imagine surviving in that environment. So I also sincerely thank the Innkeepers Association and all of the Innkeepers of Key West. There was not a person among the group who was not willing to help us at any crossroad, give advice, or simply lend a sympathetic shoulder. Thank you all.

Thank you to Mandy Bolen for editing this book. I have long admired your writing and am still in awe that you edited mine. Thank you to Rob O'Neal for the photography. Again, I have always loved your pictures of everything, particularly Cuba, and feel so fortunate to have your talent added to these pages. Thank you to Jodi Bombace for your diligent work on the layout and cover of this book. I suspect you may have spent as many hours on this manuscript as I have.

Finally, thank you to Phantom Press. A first book is not an easy venture and most publishers do not like to take a chance. Happily, for me, you guys are different from the average publisher. Very different. In a really good way. I can't say thank you enough for giving me this opportunity.

Also available from Phantom Press
www.phantompress.com

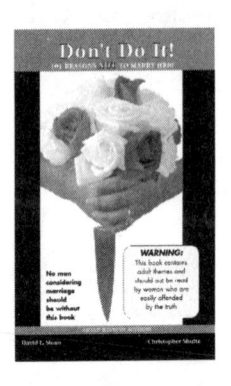

Also available from Phantom Press
www.phantompress.com

*What are you waiting for?
Open a guest house already!*